Praise for *It Sto*

"It Stops Now! is the mos. ...prehensive and practical book on harassment and bullying I have seen. It is an invaluable resource for all those who are committed to working towards eradicating harassment and bullying behaviours.

"The author enables the reader to gain a full understanding of what constitutes harassment and bullying and then outlines clear ways of dealing with the issues within the laws of the UK, Ireland USA, Canada, Australia and New Zealand.

"Josie Hastings uses her vast knowledge, expertise and experience of the subject to produce this exceptionally useable guide and resource book which is of great value & use to a range of individuals & organisations."

– Jeni G, Trainer, lecturer, and counsellor

"I have frequently used the advice in Josie Hastings's book *It Stops Now!* to address and successfully overcome issues of bullying and low-level disrespectful behaviour when dealing with colleagues and staff members on the different projects I've managed. Her advice is sound and helped me to create high performing and respectful teams.

"Conversely, her BIFF technique enabled me to transform my relationship with a contract manager who was bullying me, and I now have an excellent working relationship with him."

> – *Christine K, Project Manager and Executive Coach*

IT STOPS
NOW!

Everything a manager needs to know
to deal with harassment and bullying
in their team or place of work

JOSIE HASTINGS

Contents

Acknowledgements

I want to thank all the people who have helped me in writing this book.

Chris Payne who showed me how to structure the book, turning an idea in my head into reality. I am also grateful for his on-going feedback and support throughout the process.

Christine Korczak, who was my book buddy and helped me to keep going with her wonderful words of encouragement at every stage.

Ron Lamberson, my US editor and HR expert who provided valuable insight and content on the US and Canadian approach to harassment and bullying. His vast experience and enthusiasm for the subject made all the difference.

Ken Leeder, who created the perfect design for my book cover and Kate Vishnyakova for her excellent illustrations inside the book.

Farah Canicosa and Toby Payne for producing the final book layout and bringing my book to life.

I also want to thank all the business owners, directors and managers who provided testimonials and feedback including Mabel Garcia Aranda, Dr Kanwar Ratra, Dr Saaqib Ali, Marie Ruffle, Nathalie Brule, Mark Blaney, Steven Thompson and Jennifer Gray.

Last but not least, I want to thank my husband, Zoran Djurkovic, for his patience and support while I was writing the book.

About the Author

Josie has been a trainer, adviser and coach helping managers and business owners to deal with harassment, bullying and disrespectful behaviour in their workplaces for over 25 years.

She is a recognised expert in the area of harassment and bullying and has worked for many organisations, both large corporations and small businesses across all sectors of employment. More recently she was appointed as the external harassment and bullying guardian for the Royal College of Anaesthetists.

To my US and Canadian readers. I am based in the UK so have used UK English in this book which spells some words differently. For example, behaviour instead of behavior, colour instead of color, organisation instead of organization and victimisation instead of victimization. Please don't be distracted by this.

I worked with a US-based editor and HR expert in developing this book to ensure that the US and Canadian perspective on this subject was accurately presented.

Free Gift!

As a "thank-you" for getting this book, I'd like to give you some free gifts.

Unique pdf reports called:

- The 10 steps to take when your employee says they're being bullied or harassed

- 10 key steps for carrying out a harassment investigation in the US

- 10 key steps for carrying out a harassment or bullying investigation in the UK

Go here to get the three reports:

https://josiehastings.co.uk/HarassmentReports

Enjoy!

Contact Details

Please feel free to contact Josie Hastings to ask any questions or for more information.

Email: josiehastings@gmail.com
Phone: +44 1922 643330
Mobile: +44 7957 870294

If you would like more information on her harassment and bullying face-to-face, virtual and online training courses, go to:

Website: www.josiehastings.co.uk
Facebook: JHA Online

What her clients say about her

"I have had the pleasure of knowing Josie since 2010. I have always found her courses and training in bullying and harassment and equality and diversity second to none.

"Her attention to detail and interactive training proves for a reliable and entertaining education that allows implementation in real-life situations immediately.

"Furthermore, outside her courses and training the support she has offered sets her apart from others.

"Nothing is ever too much trouble for her, and she has to be the most helpful person I have ever come across.

"Being able to rely on her and use her wealth of knowledge and advice across my multiple businesses is something I could now not do without!"

– Dr Kanwar Ratra, Director Sentra Medical Limited, Principal Dental Surgeon and Proprietor, Landsdowne Dental Practice

"Josie has been the go-to person for employment advice in the Midlands for dental practices since 2008. She is the industry expert trusted by Health Education England to train and advise on bullying and harassment issues.

"Her calm and measured approach is backed by a wealth of knowledge and is extremely reassuring. She has also been available by phone or email to offer me tailored one to one advice that is specific to my workplace."

– Dr Saaqib Ali, Principal Dental Surgeon and Proprietor

"We have worked with Josie since 2010. In an industry where harassment, bullying and equality can be alien terms, Josie delivers practical, relatable and engaging training sessions for our staff and managers. She manages to graciously connect behaviours at work with real implications for employees and employers. Her sessions are memorable and the right mix of lightness and seriousness.

"Outside of her training, Josie is always available to answer questions and help us to deal with issues on a one-to-one basis. We are proud to work with her and delighted she has put her experience in a book for all."

– Mabel Garcia Aranda, People Culture & EDI Manager, Ferrovial Construction

"Josie designs and runs an extensive dignity and respect programme for all our staff and managers using her team of actor-coaches. The programme is very successful, and she runs a yearly refresher course; always adapting her programme to the latest context and issues.

"She also set up our Staff Supporters programme to ensure that our staff have access to trained people if they feel they are being bullied or harassed. Josie was instrumental in helping us design the policy, selection process and training for the Supporters.

The programme of Staff Supporters is well embedded at the Inn, thanks to her pragmatic approach. Josie is very approachable, and our employees respond well to her.

"The courses she runs are exceptionally well received, and lead to changes in employee behaviours. Josie is excellent at listening and taking on board complex ideas and then presenting them clearly and concisely. She is very easy to work with and brings a lot of experience to the table."

– Natalie Brule, HR Director, Honourable Society of Lincoln's Inn

"Josie Hastings was recommended to us in 2015 to run Dignity and Respect Training for all our staff and managers. Her sessions using actor-coaches were thought-provoking, entirely appropriate for our audience and well-received by all who attended.

"We then engaged her for our Staff Representative training. This role was created to empower and train some of our employees to help staff regarding any work-related dignity and respect concerns they may have. After a discussion on our requirements, Josie provided us with the role profile and skills set required for the role. Josie presented to our whole staff group to explain the role and encourage staff to apply. We had many volunteers. She interviewed all the respondents to appoint the most appropriate individuals and provided training for all those chosen.

"Josie continues to work for us to this day. We have appointed new volunteers as staff have left, and she provides the same service.

"Josie goes beyond the call of duty, making herself available outside of training sessions to answer any further questions from our staff representatives. She has a down-to-earth personality and knows how to get the best from people."

– Marie Ruffle, HR Manager, Keble College, Oxford University

"In 2019, the College appointed Josie Hastings as our Guardian of Safe Working. This role is independent of the management structure of the College. It provides staff with a safe conduit to report concerns regarding bullying, harassment, workload issues and any other matters that may impact on their wellbeing. In addition, Josie has provided training support to the College on equality, harassment and bullying issues since 2013 for both our employees and volunteers.

She is also currently a proactive member of the College's Equality Committee. Her expert contribution is informed by a wealth of experience and has definitely contributed positively to the College's work. Josie is both approachable and friendly and can put our staff and volunteers at ease when discussing sensitive and complex matters.

> *– Mark Blaney, Finance and Resources Director,*
> *Royal College of Anaesthetists*

"Josie Hastings has delivered equality and inclusion training with her team of actor-coaches for our organisation since 2015.

"She is one of those extraordinary people who know how to engage with an audience. The simple way in which Josie shares knowledge and information always leaves you wanting more."

> *– Steven Thompson, Workforce Development*
> *Manager, The National Lottery Heritage Fund*

Part One: Harassment and Bullying – Definitions, Examples, Consequences and Liabilities

Chapter 1

Why do you need this toolkit?

Harassment and bullying.

If you manage people, these are words you probably dread.

You're not alone; most managers feel the same.

Why? Because, apart from the obvious actions, harassment and bullying incidents are open to different interpretations.

Where do you draw the line between what's acceptable and unacceptable behaviour at work?

You'll have observed that jokes or 'banter' enjoyed by one employee are seen as offensive by another.

Or you manage a poorly performing employee in a supportive way and they accuse you of bullying them.

If your employee tells you they're being harassed or bullied, what are you supposed to do?

How should you respond to that first approach?

You know that saying or doing the wrong thing at the outset risks making things worse.

And if you manage a complaint poorly, it could undermine your team's trust in you.

And, to top it all, you and your organisation could be held legally responsible if you make a mess of it.

No wonder it's easier to bury your head in the sand and hope it goes away!

Unfortunately, it won't, and the longer you wait to deal with it, the worse it will get.

If it does blow up into a significant incident, you could find yourself involved in a financially costly Employment Tribunal or Court case.

Even if it doesn't go that far, you could face serious ramifications. Some of your staff may leave. Then they could trash you or your company's reputation by spreading negative stories online, which costs you in other ways.

What's the answer?

If you manage staff and have any of these concerns, this toolkit is for you.

The toolkit is in two parts. The first part captures the precarious landscape of harassment and bullying. The second part equips you to take control and survive allegations or incidents.

Part One: Harassment and bullying – definitions, examples, consequences and liabilities

In Part One, you'll learn:

- How harassment and bullying are defined in the United Kingdom (UK), the Republic of Ireland (ROI), Australia, New Zealand (NZ), Canada and the United States (US).

- What the law says about harassment and bullying in these six countries.

- The implications for you, your business and employees.

- The many forms of harassment and bullying, both obvious and subtle, so you'll recognise them when you see them.

- What behaviours are <u>not</u> harassment and bullying.

- The impact of harassment and bullying on individuals, your team and your organisation, if you don't deal with it.

Part Two: Preventing and dealing with harassment and bullying at work

In Part Two, you'll learn the techniques and strategies that will help you to address harassment and bullying in your workplace. You will learn:

- Ways to respond to complaints from your staff, including what to say and what not to say.

- A process for addressing inappropriate behaviour you can teach your staff.

- How to deal with the bully or harasser when you receive a complaint.

- How to address passive-aggressive behaviours within your team.

- Ways to minimise the risk of harassment and bullying arising in the first place.

- The steps you can take to create a more respectful workplace culture.

All of the above will benefit your business, organisation or practice, and make your life less stressful too!

Chapter 2

The benefits of getting it right

What happens when your staff are hit by a harassment or bullying incident?

The impact is often widespread. Dealing with harassment and bullying effectively will not only help you avoid irreparable harm, it will help your bottom line and profits.

Here's how:

More productive employees

Your staff are more productive and engaged when they feel safe at work.

They work harder when they're free of problems with co-workers or managers, and they're more willing to help and support colleagues, which means they'll provide a better service to your customers, clients or patients.

Less sickness absence

When your employees are happy at work, they take less time off sick.

Loyalty and retention

Turnover is expensive. Recruiting and training new staff is costly in both time and money.

You want to hold on to your best people.

When your staff feel respected, appreciated and listened to, they're more likely to stay with your organisation.

Greater contribution from your team

Create a workplace where your employees feel valued and respected, and they'll:

- Contribute more to your business
- Have the space to be innovative and creative
- Help you to solve problems when they arise.

The consequences of getting it wrong

The human cost

Harassment and bullying can have a devastating and long-lasting effect on your staff. They feel anxious, intimidated, or fearful at work.

Feelings of anger and frustration create stress, resulting in time off due to sickness.

Your staff may lose motivation which decreases their work performance.

All of which impacts on you and your business.

Over time, targets of harassment and bullying lose confidence and self-esteem. If they leave their job (as many do), it's harder for them to find another job.

In extreme cases, the trauma has led to self-harm and suicide.

Legal consequences

Your staff can take legal action against you or your company if they are harassed or bullied in your workplace.

Complainants have been awarded compensation running into thousands of pounds, dollars or euros for successful claims of harassment and bullying at work.

31

The legal fees involved in defending a claim are considerable too. As a result, you may have to settle a claim 'out of court', just to avoid the costs of litigation.

Disruption

Although most complaints don't escalate to legal action, they can take up a lot of time. The hours spent in meetings and interviews sap your productivity.

Everyone involved is thrown off balance. The disruption to your workplace could take months to overcome.

Damage to reputation

Bad news travels at the speed of light. Stories about what went on and by whom, spread rapidly, particularly on social media outlets such as Glassdoor.

This negative publicity damages your reputation and the reputations of your team, department or organisation.

Job seekers rely on the gossip they uncover online. Reports of a hostile work environment or routine bullying can cripple your future recruitment campaigns.

You play a huge role in getting it right. You need to strengthen your situational awareness – accept and be conscious that your staff are closely watching everything you say and do.

Making respectful behaviour a priority will build your reputation as an effective leader.

Chapter 3

What does the law say about harassment and bullying?

If you have employees in:

- United Kingdom (UK)
- Republic of Ireland (ROI)
- United States (US)
- Canada
- Australia
- New Zealand (NZ)

...then they are protected by anti-discrimination legislation.

Harassment

Harassment is a form of discrimination in these countries. The behaviour must have a link to your employee's protected characteristic, grounds or class (explained later in this chapter) to be covered by discrimination legislation.

Intent and impact

When you are trying to identify and manage incidents, the way the law approaches these situations may surprise you.

Firstly, harassment doesn't need to be deliberate to be unlawful or illegal.

Your employee may not have intended to harass their colleague. But it is the impact on the recipient that is considered significant in these situations.

Secondly, the terms unwanted and unwelcome appear in the harassment definitions of several countries.

You probably think this means the recipient would have to tell the perpetrator or you, their manager, that they objected to the behaviour. Otherwise, how would you know?

Wrong!

A recipient does not have to say they object to the behaviour for it to be considered unwanted, legally.

Conduct can be unwelcome, even if an employee submits to it, or puts up with it.

Your employee may not speak up for various reasons:

- they are concerned about being viewed as a 'trouble-maker', or

- they are afraid of retaliation by the offender, or

- think they'll lose their job if they challenge someone senior to them, or

- they're unsure how to make a complaint.

Saying that you didn't know the behaviour was unwanted or unwelcome by the complainant is not a defence.

Witnesses to inappropriate behaviour can make complaints

One of your employees could witness behaviour that they find intimidating, hostile, degrading, or offensive.

In these situations, they can claim harassment or bullying, even though the actions were not directed at them.

Legal definitions of harassment and bullying

The laws defining harassment and bullying in the UK, ROI, the US, Canada, Australia and NZ are in Appendix A at the back of the toolkit.

Outlined below, as an illustration, are the legal definitions for:

- harassment in the UK and US

- bullying in Australia and the UK.

Harassment definitions

United Kingdom UK (Equality Act 2010)

'Unwanted conduct that has the purpose or effect of either violating another person's dignity or creating an intimidating, hostile, degrading, humiliating or offensive environment for that person.'

To be unlawful, there must be a link to the employee's protected characteristic which, in the UK, are: age, disability, gender reassignment; race, religion and belief, sex, or sexual orientation.

United States US (Title VII Civil Rights Act 1964)

'Unwelcome conduct that is a condition of continued employment or that creates an intimidating, hostile, or offensive work environment.'

Harassment is illegal when an employee is mistreated because they are a member of a protected class, which are age, disability, race, colour, ethnicity, religion, sex (including pregnancy), and national origin.

Also, several US states such as Minnesota and California, have their own anti-discrimination laws protecting employees within other classes, such as sexual orientation or gender identity.

Bullying definitions

Laws in the UK, ROI, NZ, US and Canada expressly prohibit bullying, as with harassment, only when it's linked to an employee's protected characteristic.

Some jurisdictions in the US and Canada include bullying under the term, 'hostile work environment.' Australia applies a broader standard.

Australia (Fair Work Amendment Act 2013)

In Australia, the Fair Work Amendment Act 2013 defines bullying as:

'Repeated unreasonable behaviour by an individual towards a worker which creates a risk to health and safety.

'Bullying is when people repeatedly and intentionally use words or actions against someone or a group of people to cause distress and risk to their well-being.'

Employees don't have to link the behaviour to their protected characteristic, grounds or class to make a legal claim, as is required in other countries.

United Kingdom (ACAS Code of Practice)

In the UK, employers are expected to implement the guidance in the ACAS Code of Practice which defines bullying as:

'Offensive, intimidating, malicious or insulting behaviour which intentionally or unintentionally undermines, humiliates, denigrates or injures the recipient.'

Definitions of victimisation or retaliation

Countries with anti-discrimination legislation also prohibit victimisation in the UK, ROI, Australia and NZ; called retaliation in the US and Canada.

These terms have a specific meaning in this legislation. They are defined similarly in each country as taking action to penalise an employee who, in good faith, has:

- made allegations or complaints of harassment or bullying, or
- helped other employees who are making a complaint
  - o by providing evidence
  - o participating in an investigation
  - o acting as a witness.

Chapter 4

What behaviours are harassment and bullying?

Many behaviours could fall under the definitions of harassment and bullying. In an ideal world, you would have an exhaustive list of practices or actions to look out for, avoid or challenge.

In reality, it's more complicated.

Context and perception

Often the same actions or comments from two different people in your team will lead to very different responses from the recipient.

Whether one of your employees is offended, humiliated, embarrassed, intimidated or upset by another employee's behaviour depends on many factors.

The context in which behaviour occurs influences how appropriate or reasonable the perpetrator's actions are viewed.

Relationship between colleagues

Friendships function differently than workplace relationships. If your employee likes and trusts a colleague, they may not mind them making personal comments or jokes at their expense. They've built a rapport that makes them feel safe.

Conversely, if a colleague whom they don't like or trust did or said the same thing, they could be offended. When employees are oblivious to that need for trust, they can easily cross the line.

Level of seniority

Your employee making a jokey comment about a colleague on the same job grade being 'hopeless at spreadsheets' might be laughed off or agreed with.

A manager making or laughing at the same comment may have a different impact.

The employee could interpret the manager's action as undermining and an attempt to humiliate them in front of their colleagues.

If the manager's behaviour is repeated, your employee could make a complaint.

Cultural differences

You probably employ staff who originate from countries across the world. Employees from diverse backgrounds and cultures are a great asset to any business or organisation.

You need to be prepared for their varied perspectives of what is considered 'normal' workplace behaviour.

Behaviours in your team considered acceptable by employees from one country or culture may be viewed as inappropriate by employees from another.

For example, some employees may hug or kiss each other on the cheek when they've not met up for a while. Other employees would be horrified if a colleague tried to hug or kiss them on the cheek, regardless of how close they were!

41

Employees who share the same heritage may be comfortable using slang or terminology amongst themselves, which would be considered grossly offensive if used by anyone from a different culture.

It's easy for other employees to misunderstand these situations and think it's OK to use the same terminology or behave in the same manner.

This form of cultural appropriation*, even when conducted with positive intent, can result in significant misunderstandings or even conflict.

*The unacknowledged or inappropriate adoption of the customs, practices, ideas, of one people or society by members of another and typically more dominant people or society.

Respectful communication

In some countries or cultures, it's common practice to 'soften' instructions to staff and colleagues.

You and your team add words and phrases to show you're 'polite' or 'respectful', such as:

- "would you mind doing this as soon as you're free?"
- "is it OK if I interrupt you for a moment?"

Also adding "please" and "thank you" to all requests would be the expectation.

For staff from cultures where a direct approach is the workplace norm, this sounds strange. "I need you to do this now" would be more appropriate.

And saying 'please' and 'thank you' would be considered irrelevant when giving an instruction.

If colleagues come from a culture where a 'polite tone' to show respect is the norm, a direct approach may sound abrupt or rude.

Not everyone can adapt to a change in communication style.

Make sure you let your employees know your expectations and provide guidance if required.

Voice tone and body language

You may employ staff from countries or cultures where it's usual for people to:

- speak loudly

- use very expressive body language

- sit or stand very close to colleagues when having a discussion.

Your employees from less expressive cultures may interpret this behaviour as:

- being shouted out at

- being threatened or intimidated

- thinking their colleague is 'invading their personal space'.

Be mindful of those who have a style that tends to clash with your team's cultural norms. Guide them to help minimise potential friction. Small concessions from both parties can improve the work environment.

The culture of the organisation you work in

If you've worked for several different companies or organisations, you'll have noticed that workplace cultures vary enormously.

The culture of individual departments within the same organisation can also be quite different.

To keep matters simple, workplace cultures have been categorised into four main types:

The **clan culture** which is based on collaboration.

- Managers actively support their employees with coaching and mentoring
- Teamwork, communication and consensus are valued.

The **adhocracy culture** which is based on ideas and innovation.

- Management is very 'hands-off'
- Employees are valued for their ingenuity and creativity and encouraged to take risks.

The **market culture** which is goal-oriented, competitive and results-driven.

- It values market share and profitability
- Employees have demanding targets and are measured on performance.

The **hierarchy culture** which is formal.

- It is based on structure and control
- Employees are valued for their efficiency, consistency and uniformity.

Behaviours considered acceptable in a market culture are likely to be seen as unacceptable in a clan culture.

For example, how performance issues are addressed.

In a market culture, a manager might arrange formal meetings immediately with a staff member who'd not met their sales targets on three occasions in a short space of time.

They issue formal warnings at each meeting, and the employee is told they'll be dismissed if they fail to meet their targets on a fourth occasion. No additional guidance or support is offered to the employee.

In a clan culture, an employee's performance would be addressed informally at first.

Additional guidance, training or coaching would be provided to support the employee to meet the required standards over an extended period.

Formal meetings would not be considered until the manager felt they were unavoidable.

Adapting to the workplace culture

A new employee will usually bring the behaviours that were acceptable in their previous workplace with them.

If your team has a very different culture, this could cause problems. You have an opportunity to anticipate these differences by:

- setting out accurate expectations within the recruitment process

- covering the expected behavioural standards during induction to your team.

Fortunately, most new employees recognise the need to adapt very early on. They modify their behaviour to fit in with the cultural expectations.

Others may find it difficult to change and could create conflict in your team if this is not addressed.

Workplace alliances

Research has shown that workplace friendships improve employee engagement. Members of your team will form bonds with colleagues who share common interests or backgrounds. It's human nature.

In contrast, they may avoid a colleague whom they perceive as 'different'.

Their difference could be in terms of age, gender, race, religion, sexuality, lifestyle, or because they have a disability. Or because the team feel they have 'nothing in common' with their co-worker.

Your staff may avoid engaging with them in breaks or at lunch. They feel justified because, from their perspective, they 'don't know what to talk about with their colleague' or they fear they'll 'say the wrong thing' and offend them.

It won't take long for your staff member to realise they're being excluded. If they think they 'don't belong' they are more likely to leave their job.

Implications

The next section focuses on behaviours typically seen as harassment and bullying.

Some are clearly unacceptable in any organisation, regardless of context. Others are not so clear-cut.

Context or perception will influence whether or not your employees see them as harassment or bullying.

Remember, harassment and bullying can occur face-to-face, by phone, or in written or electronic communications.

Examples of harassment

Behaviours viewed as harassment include:

- unwelcome physical contact, unnecessary touching or brushing against another person's body or physical assault

- coercing sexual acts or repeated invitations for dates or meetings outside of the workplace

- persistently sending unwanted gifts

- following, spying on, or stalking someone

- physical threats or attacks

- insulting or abusive behaviours or gestures

- invading someone's 'personal space'

49

- unwelcome verbal conduct, such as:

  o making remarks about personal appearance

  o lewd comments

  o sexual advances

  o innuendos

- giving people nicknames or name-calling

- automatically anglicising 'foreign-sounding' names

- making fun of someone or telling inappropriate jokes

- workplace 'banter' which upsets some team members

- making offensive or stereotyped comments to, or about, a person

- intrusive personal questioning regarding, (eg, a colleague's sexual orientation or religious beliefs) directly with the individual, or with others, about the individual

- unwelcome written or visual interaction, such as:

  o sending unwanted and/or inappropriate notes or pictures

  o displaying offensive material on notice boards or wall space.

Examples of bullying

Bullying typically includes:

- physical violence or threats of violence

- shouting or screaming

- using profane or abusive language

- threats about an employee's job security, or intimidation

- disparaging, ridiculing or mocking remarks

- making an employee's working life unreasonably difficult by:

  o setting impossible targets

  o continually changing objectives

  o setting an excessive workload or unrealistic deadlines

  o removing areas of responsibility without reason or explanation

  o refusing requests for training or development opportunities without good reason

  o blocking an employee's advancement without cause.

Cyber bullying or harassment

Most business communication happens electronically.

Your staff may not be subject to harassment or bullying in person but may be affected by cyberbullying or harassment.

This behaviour occurs through instant messaging or chat, text messages, email and social networking sites or forums.

Examples of cyberbullying include:

- sending derogatory, obscene, or insulting texts or emails

- copying other employees into emails that are critical or highlight a person's mistakes

- posting offensive written or visual content

- threatening or blackmailing a person via social media

- distributing photographs, videos or recordings of individuals, gained illicitly

- misrepresenting someone, eg using their Facebook or Instagram accounts to post inappropriate messages as if it were them

- trolling a person.

Covert or indirect forms of harassment and bullying

Most workplaces have progressed away from the more overt forms of harassment and bullying.

Behaviour such as assaults, physical threats, unwanted touching or groping, coercion for sexual favours, screaming or swearing at employees or colleagues is not tolerated, and less frequent.

However, these obvious behaviours have been replaced by more covert and indirect forms of harassment or bullying. These are often referred to, collectively, as passive-aggressive behaviours and they can be the most destructive.

Passive-aggressive behaviours include:

- withholding information
- put-downs in meetings
- making sarcastic comments
- microaggressions
- gaslighting
- spreading rumours or gossip

- work or social exclusion.

These behaviours are difficult to identify because they are subtle. Even when you do notice them; you may not acknowledge them as harassment or bullying at first.

These behaviours are destructive at work because they can continue unabated. If you fail to address them or dismiss them as 'workplace politics', they will undermine the morale and well-being of your team.

Put-downs and sarcastic comments or conduct

Put-downs, insults and sarcastic comments can happen in a range of workplace settings. You may have observed them in meetings, in conversations between work colleagues during work time, or during breaks.

The perpetrators who rely on insults are often clever. They avoid blatant put-downs and are adept at making comments that fly under your radar.

You may not address their comments because you're not sure they meant what they said, or if you heard it correctly. The target, however, rarely misinterprets the insult.

Sarcasm is contagious. One of your employees makes a sarcastic remark; another joins in the fun. Employees who use sarcasm like to hide under the veil of humour.

In well-functioning teams, a small amount of sarcasm provides valuable levity, but it's a slippery slope. You need to control it if it gets taken too far.

Microaggressions

Microaggressions are brief denigrating comments or actions directed to a person because they belong to a particular group. They usually relate to their protected characteristic such as their age, disability, gender identity, race, religion, sex or sexuality.

Microaggressions can range from well-intentioned, but offensive, questions and comments to nuanced discrimination.

A list of common microaggressions is included in Appendix B.

If you are unfamiliar with the term here are some examples you may recognise.

Towards employees from minority ethnic groups

- Q: Where are you from? A: London. Q: But where are you really from?

- It's hard to pronounce your name, so we'll call you Sue/ Sid.

- You sound white/ You don't sound black.

Towards female employees

- As you have a young family, I didn't think you'd want the extra responsibility.

- We need someone in the role who can make tough decisions.

- Kelly, can you take the meeting notes/ get the coffees for us?

Towards LGBT+ employees

- When did you know you were gay/ lesbian/ trans?
- If you're not a man or a woman, what are you then?
- It's such a waste you're gay/ lesbian.

Towards employees who have a faith

- You're not like most Muslims/ Sikhs/ Catholics/ Jews.
- Don't you have to marry someone who is the same religion?
- Don't you get hot wearing all those clothes?

Towards employees who are disabled

- You are so brave.
- I read that XX is really good for your condition. Have you tried it?
- You're taking that parking space from someone who really needs it.

Towards older/younger people

- Do you want me to help you with that iPhone/ tablet/ laptop/ new program?
- I think it's great you still work/ drive/ walk to work/ cycle to work.

- You'll understand when you've had a bit more life experience.

Microaggressions aren't limited to comments. Body language, facial expressions, vocal tone, and eye contact also fall into this category, for example:

- a manager uses a condescending tone when talking to a team member

- an employee 'roll her eyes' when her colleague makes suggestions in a meeting

- a male employee looks every woman up and down (elevator eyes) when they enter the room

- a team member sits with her back to her colleague.

These physical behaviours are even more challenging to spot and address.

An isolated insult or microaggression is not considered serious enough to be challenged by your employee, let alone complained about.

The remarks may not be reported as harassment or bullying until they've gone on for a long time.

At this stage, your employee may:

- think it's too late to challenge, so puts up with it, creating stress for themselves

- believe it's impossible to provide sufficient evidence of inappropriate behaviour to complain due to its subtlety

- feel resentful towards the colleague who makes the remarks, which erodes their working relationship over time

- decide that they're not accepted in the team so starts to look for another job

- tells other people who share their protected characteristic how disrespectful the work environment is, which may deter them from applying for positions in your team or department.

Gaslighting

Gaslighting is when one employee, colleague or manager manipulates another to doubt their perspective of reality.

Examples of gaslighting behaviour include:

- denying your employee said or did something when they did (or vice versa)

- using personal information to undermine or humiliate them

- criticising their actions, work, words or ability to do their job in private or public.

Gaslighting happens slowly, eventually wearing down your employee's self-esteem.

A frequent sign that your employee may be a target is an increase in self-doubt, such as:

- apologising often

- difficulty making decisions

- feeling isolated from work colleagues

- feeling more anxious or less confident

- thinking they're doing everything wrong.

Mobbing

Mobbing is a term that describes a group of employees joining together to harass or bully a colleague.

Managers are increasingly becoming targets of mobbing. Some employers use the term to describe all forms of harassment and bullying against managers.

It is not indirect or covert behaviour. It's included in this section because it's frequently not acknowledged or dealt with effectively in the workplace.

Mobbing of managers is particularly prevalent in workplaces where staff are in high-status roles – think highly respected academics or doctors, long-term employees or high-producing sales professionals.

Individuals in these roles often resent being managed by anyone. In particular, someone they see as having less knowledge or expertise than they possess.

Mobbing is also common when a colleague is promoted to manage a team in which they used to be a member.

Or where the team recognise their manager is inexperienced and take advantage of the situation.

Mobbing behaviours by employees include:

- refusal to carry out instructions
- refusal to adhere to expected standards on timekeeping, attending meetings, submitting paperwork, attending mandatory training
- disruptive behaviour in meetings
- constantly challenging views, suggestions or ideas expressed by the manager
- making fabricated claims of inappropriate actions against their manager
- taking out constant unjustified grievances against their manager.

Mobbing should be dealt with in the same way as other forms of harassment and bullying.

Unfortunately, in many workplaces, it is not, because:

- no-one is prepared to confront the behaviour of the 'high value' employee
- the manager is fearful of being viewed as weak or incompetent for not being able to manage their team
- the employees' complaints demonstrate to senior managers that the manager is the wrong person to lead that team.

Often managers feel too ashamed to make complaints about being harassed or bullied by their team or an individual. They choose to leave rather than speak up.

Fortunately, more enlightened employers recognise mobbing as a problem.

They have adapted their procedures to acknowledge that managers can be harassed or bullied, and how to report it.

Exclusion

Exclusion is challenging to address.

Recipients find it hard to speak up about behaviour which is passive and based on the absence of action, eg everyone in the team blanks me at work.

For those who feel excluded, a complaint can seem petty or childish.

We'll dedicate ample time to addressing exclusion in Chapter 11.

Chapter 5

What behaviours are not harassment or bullying?

Eradicating harassment and bullying in your team is hard enough.

What happens when your employees label reasonable or acceptable work behaviours as bullying or harassment?

These complaints frequently occur when staff members disagree with your management practices.

You need to be equipped to respond effectively.

Reasonable management actions

You are free to manage your staff appropriately, which means you can and should:

- assign tasks and responsibilities to your team

- issue reasonable instructions and expect that they'll be carried out

- set and publicise expected standards of performance

- provide regular and relevant feedback to your staff on their performance

- carry out appraisals

- manage your employees' attendance

- provide guidance, coaching or training for your employees if you have capability concerns

- discipline staff for misconduct, where appropriate, following a fair and proper investigation.

You will be required to address performance issues with your staff from time to time.

Most employees will feel anxious when you take them through these procedures. You should ensure they are:

- administered in private and kept confidential

- based on facts and evidence relating to your employee's actions

- carried out in a supportive manner – which may require the provision of further guidance, coaching, mentoring or training for your employee.

However, if in carrying out these procedures, you:

- reprimand your employee in front of other staff

- engage in conversations with other team members about their 'failings'

- betray their confidences

- are not able to back up your discussion with actual evidence of under-performance

- make personal attacks

- don't follow your organisation's procedures.

Your actions are likely to be seen as bullying or harassing behaviour.

Other behaviours that are not harassment or bullying

A single or isolated incident

It's impossible to predict 100% of the time what might upset, embarrass or offend a colleague or member of your team. No matter how sensitive you are to the feelings of others, you'll get it wrong sometimes.

What happens when you make that one regrettable comment?

What is important is how you respond when you realise or are told you have offended, embarrassed or upset someone.

If your employee objects to what you said or did, you could decide they're being 'over-sensitive' or 'taking things out of perspective' and react defensively.

You may make matters worse by launching into a justification of what you said; how they misinterpreted what you said; reminding them of inappropriate things they've said to you in the past.

Not the best response.

Instead, take a deep breath, remember it's better to stop these situations from escalating and say something along the lines of:

- It was not my intention/ the last thing on my mind to offend/ upset/ undermine/ embarrass you

- I apologise for what I said/ did. I am sorry for offending/ upsetting/ undermining/ embarrassing you.

When you, or your employee, acknowledge that the other person is upset and make a genuine apology, then a one-off incident would not be harassment or bullying.

Even if the other employee tries to pursue it further to make a point, it's unlikely the complaint would hold merit.

Differences of opinion

In your workplace, it may be commonplace for your employees to have robust discussions or disagreements regarding work matters.

These might relate to the merits of business strategies, outcomes of research, or ideas for new products or services. They are part of the normal process of validating a project or idea.

Sometimes the employee 'feels bullied' if the strategy, research or idea they are presenting is challenged. Differing opinions are not viewed as harassment or bullying.

However, you need to make sure these discussions don't devolve into harassment or bullying.

If an opposing employee makes a personal attack or argues unprofessionally, you need to intervene.

Pressure or stress of work

There will be times when the workload is more intense than usual, or your team has tight deadlines to meet.

Your staff may struggle in these circumstances and complain of harassment and bullying.

As long as this is not a regular occurrence, it would not be viewed as workplace harassment or bullying.

However, uninterrupted periods of increased workload, long hours or impossible deadlines could trigger a valid complaint of bullying.

It is more likely to lead to a complaint if it is only one or two team members who are facing these pressures.

Be careful of overloading staff members who are efficient workers when you are under pressure.

Difficult conditions of employment, professional constraints and organisational changes

An office location changes.

A new, unknown manager is brought in from the outside.

A job function is eliminated or outsourced.

Your staff may not be happy with any of these. However, they would not be viewed as harassment or bullying.

It is difficult to diffuse these situations as neither you nor your staff can change what's happened. Shifting your employees focus onto issues you or they could influence may be more productive.

Friends and more than friends

Your employees are human. They will form social, or sometimes, romantic relationships with each other.

When your employees are friends, or in a relationship, they will tolerate comments or behaviour that would not be acceptable from other staff in the team.

If they fall out with each other, that level of tolerance may change dramatically.

Either employee may come to you and complain about instances of previously accepted behaviours and attempt to use these to make a claim of harassment or bullying against their former friend or partner.

This is one of the reasons why some companies try (unsuccessfully) to ban employees from having relationships with their colleagues!

These breakdowns in friendship or relationships can be fraught and cause significant problems at work. You would need to tread carefully in assessing the evidence presented, taking into consideration the 'history' between the two of them.

If you become aware of a relationship ending, you may want to have a private discussion with both parties proactively.

This enables you to confirm the change and document when it occurred and can eliminate the 'backdating' of violations.

Frivolous, vexatious or malicious complaints

Your employees may make trivial, unfounded or fabricated complaints, causing problems for you or your staff. (Go to Appendix C for definitions and examples.)

Employees who do so are not protected from victimisation or retaliation laws and may warrant disciplinary action.

However, beware! Proving complaints are frivolous, vexatious or malicious is extremely difficult.

If your employee made the complaint 'in good faith', which means they genuinely believed their complaint was valid, then it would not fall under this definition.

It can be challenging to convince an Employment Tribunal or Court that an employee has absolutely no basis for their complaint.

Chapter 6

Who is liable – employee or employer?

As an employer, you are legally responsible for acts of harassment or bullying that occur in your workplace.

The legal term used in the UK, ROI, Australia and NZ, for this responsibility is 'vicarious liability'. In Canada and the US, 'employer liability' is used.

When does this liability begin?

Your employees do not have full employment rights until they have been in your employment for a qualifying period. These vary from country to country and can last up to two years.

However, in a claim of discrimination, harassment or bullying, qualifying periods do not apply.

This means that your employees can take legal action against you from day one.

Where and when are you liable?

You can also be held liable for harassment that occurs 'in connection with a person's employment'.

This means you're responsible for incidents that take place:

- during work-related social functions such as Christmas or other workplace parties (even if your staff organised these without your knowledge)

- at external training courses or conferences sponsored by your organisation

- on business or field trips when employees socialise with each other after working hours.

Your liability can extend to staff using workplace computers, phones or tablets to harass another employee outside of work.

They could do this by:

- sending offensive texts or email messages

- sharing inappropriate videos

- posting derogatory comments about colleagues or managers on social media sites.

Personal liability

What about the responsibility of the person who was directly involved in the incident?

You'll be relieved to know that individuals who harass or bully their work colleagues are, of course, directly liable for their personal actions.

You have the right to discipline and terminate these employees.

More extreme incidents of harassment and bullying can lead to criminal charges against the perpetrator, resulting in fines or even imprisonment.

Is my company doing the right things?

The good news is that you can minimise your liability in two specific ways, by:

- demonstrating that you've taken 'all reasonable steps' to prevent harassment from occurring in your workplace, and

- showing that you've responded appropriately to resolve incidents of harassment when they have occurred.

When you can show clear evidence of these actions, the perpetrator alone would be held liable for their behaviour.

If you can't demonstrate you've taken all reasonable steps?

Then it's likely both your organisation and the employee perpetrating the behaviour would be legally liable.

All parties are typically required to pay financial compensation to successful complainants in Employment Tribunals or Courts.

How can you show you took 'all reasonable steps?'

Anti-discrimination laws do not provide a clear-cut definition of 'all reasonable steps'.

What is deemed reasonable depends on the size and resources of your organisation.

In a large corporation, you would be expected to take more steps than if you run a small business.

However, all employers, regardless of size, are expected to take active steps to minimise the risk of harassment and bullying in their workplace.

Reasonable steps

In the UK, ROI, Australia, NZ and Canada, reasonable steps would require all employers to have, as a minimum:

- Grievance and disciplinary policies which make specific reference to harassment, bullying and victimisation or retaliation

- A clear procedure for raising complaints

- A means of communicating the complaints procedure to your employees when they join the organisation.

  o Don't just give the procedure to your employees and ask them to sign that they've read and understood it. That alone is not usually sufficient. You need to show evidence that you, at least, talked them through the procedure.

US: In the US under federal law, these requirements only kick in if you have 15 or more employees.

However, check your state laws, as in at least half of US States sexual harassment laws cover employers with less than 15 employees.

Best practice

It helps if you can also show that you:

- Provide interactive training sessions face-to-face or online for all employees who manage and supervise staff. This training should include:

  o how harassment, bullying and victimisation or retaliation are defined

  o what behaviours are included in these terms

  o their responsibilities as supervisors or managers

  o what to do when an employee makes an allegation or complaint.

- Run briefing sessions for employees which explain what to do if they feel harassed, bullied or victimised.

- Ensure participants sign an attendance sheet which proves they were present at any training or briefing sessions.

A large employer would be expected to do all of the above.

Taking action to deal with allegations or incidents (The UK, ROI, Australia & NZ)

You can also demonstrate you've taken all reasonable steps by dealing with complaints in a consistent and timely manner.

Take all complaints seriously, followed by prompt action to deal with the issue raised.

Both informal and formal interventions are acceptable.

Keep notes and retain records of all actions taken when dealing with a complaint.

These notes and records are your proof and would be your defence if it escalates to legal action.

Taking action in the US and Canada – On notice

United States

When an employee brings up a harassment complaint, you and your employer, are considered to be 'on notice.'

You must respond immediately and escalate the complaint to the appropriate person in your organisation to carry out an investigation.

In a large employer, this would be Human Resources, Legal, or a designated executive.

In a small employer, this could be the business owner or a partner, a senior manager or a designated staff member.

They take over the process at this point.

As the complainant's manager, you are likely to be interviewed as part of any investigation.

You will also play a role in determining any disciplinary action on completion of the investigation.

Appendix E at the back of the book explains how to carry out an investigation in the US.

Canada

In Canada, it is similar in that you are required to respond swiftly and carry out investigations into harassment claims.

However, you are also expected to offer the option of an informal resolution process.

This allows the complainant to attempt to address the behaviour informally before submitting a formal complaint.

Your employee has the option to skip or halt the informal resolution process and move to a formal complaint at any point.

Part Two:
Preventing and dealing with harassment and bullying

Chapter 7

Create a supportive environment

Creating a work environment where your staff feel respected, listened to and supported should they make a complaint, is an essential step.

On paper, you may have an excellent procedure for dealing with harassment and bullying. However, if your staff don't trust you or your organisation to implement it, then it's of little value.

Also, it's much easier for you to deal with allegations or incidents if they're brought to you in the early stages.

Staff are more likely to raise concerns if you're approachable. They need to understand that speaking up about inappropriate behaviour is an acceptable thing to do.

You can achieve this by:

- informing everyone who joins your team that you do not tolerate harassment or bullying

- explaining that the organisation has a proactive policy for dealing with issues

- ensuring they know the informal, as well as formal routes, for raising issues

- encouraging them to talk to you about their concerns at any time

- reminding them of the importance of respectful behaviour during your team briefings or meetings and during one-to-one discussions.

Identify the risk factors and warning signs in your team

Most serious incidents of harassment and bullying start with minor issues that were not addressed. You'll be better prepared if you:

- identify which of your employees are most at risk of being harassed or bullied

- recognise the warning signs that indicate a potential problem within your team.

Who is most at risk?

While any employee could be a recipient of harassment and bullying, particular members of your team are more likely to be vulnerable to inappropriate behaviour.

The 'risk factors' that make your employees vulnerable generally relate to their:

- perceived difference

- personality

- status in the workplace

- employment contract

- career stage.

Keep a watchful eye on individuals in these risk categories to ensure they're not singled out.

Perceived difference

Employees who are considered diffcrent by other members of your team are sometimes 'picked on' by colleagues. This could be because of:

- their protected characteristic, eg age, disability, gender identity, race, religion or belief, sex or sexuality

- factors such as their size, appearance, lifestyle, political views, hobbies or interests.

Their personality type

Bullies and harassers tend to target people whom they think will make easy 'victims'. They're more likely to home in on members of your team who they perceive as:

- quiet, shy or non-assertive, or

- vulnerable in some way, for example, due to personal problems or issues they're experiencing outside of work.

Hierarchy and status in the workplace

Organisational hierarchies exist in all business environments. Any employee who is in a lower position in the hierarchy or is viewed as 'less valuable' can be a prime target for inappropriate behaviour.

As you keep an eye on those who may be more susceptible to harassment or bullying, you should also monitor potential perpetrators: those who are in 'highly valued' positions.

Who falls into this highly valued category? In some organisations, it's simply the employees who occupy higher pay grades or specific titles.

In others, such as healthcare, academia, and sales, it's more complicated. Tenure, specialities, and productivity influence the value of individuals.

Either way, employees who think they're invaluable or irreplaceable, sometimes consider themselves untouchable due to:

- being the most senior person in their department or organisation
- their unique knowledge or skillset, eg medical or academic
- ability to provide revenue for the organisation in terms of: sales; customers, clients or patients; advice; attracting funding; or improving share-holder value.

Your highly valued employee may think, or in many cases know, their behaviour won't be challenged, regardless of the impact on others. Anyone who complains about, or in some instances, even displeases this individual, will be removed.

By condoning their behaviour, you're in danger of 'creating a monster', which you may regret in time.

Employees who have limited experience in the workplace

Some of your employees may have limited or no experience of the workplace before you hire them. These include:

• employees who are in their first job with your organisation

• people you employ in trainee, apprentice or intern positions.

Sometimes longer serving employees single out these individuals to make fun of them or 'initiate' them into the culture of the organisation.

They may also bombard them with menial tasks or unnecessary work simply because 'they're the intern.'

Contract status

Nowadays, employees are less likely to be hired on a continuous contract at the outset.

Some of your staff were probably recruited:

- into a temporary position

- on a fixed-term contract

- on a zero-hours or casual contract with no certainty of employment.

The 'contract status' of your staff members will influence how safe they feel in speaking up about inappropriate behaviour.

If they're hoping to gain a permanent position with you, they may keep quiet for fear of being seen as a troublemaker.

Other staff members or managers may use this to threaten or keep them quiet.

Making comments such as:

- "Your fixed-term contract ends in two months. If you want that contract renewed, is it wise to speak up/ make a complaint now?"

- "You're only a temp, not permanent staff. You don't have the same rights*."

*It's vital to inform all your employees, including temporary and casual staff, about your organisation's policies in this area.

 Let them know they have the same rights as all other employees to make complaints of harassment or bullying.

Warning signs

If you know your staff well, you're better equipped to spot the 'warning signs' that there may be issues within your team.

You may notice a change in mood or demeanour in a particular individual or see tensions between members of the team that were not there previously.

If you get into the habit of picking up on these, you can take steps to stop inappropriate behaviours from building up.

Some of the typical 'warning signs' exhibited by employees include:

- increased sickness absence as your employee wants to avoid the workplace

- withdrawal from colleagues, eg not going to breaks or lunch at the same time as colleagues

- finding excuses to be out of the office when particular colleagues are present

- no longer attending workplace social events

- not wanting to participate in meetings or training sessions, if specific individuals are present

- changes in demeanour or body language, eg facial expressions or posture, when a particular person is present, or you mention their name

- emotional outbursts such as crying or over-reaction to trivial matters

- low self-esteem in a previously confident employee

- noticing 'atmospheres' when you enter a room

- performance issues, eg you observe someone who used to perform well now can't make decisions or misses deadlines

- resignations or requests for transfers to other teams.

Where you do pick up these signs, you can address them casually with the employee concerned.

For example:

- "I often see you on your own at breaks these days. How are you getting on with the rest of the team?"

- "I noticed you stopped contributing to the discussion when X joined the meeting. How are things between the two of you?"

They may tell you that everything is OK.

You could follow this up with a comment such as

- "I'm always here if you want to discuss anything with me."

They may think about what you've said and talk to you later.

Your staff are more likely to approach you if you show you've noticed and care.

91

Chapter 8

Deal with the initial approach appropriately

For most employees, it is a big step to admit they're being bullied or harassed.

Many employees would look for another job in preference to speaking out.

Nailing your initial response

When an employee does speak up, your initial response will set the tone of the conversation.

It will influence any subsequent actions or decisions they take.

It will also be the difference between a successful or unsuccessful resolution of the situation.

Let's look at the steps you can take to make sure your initial response is regarded as helpful, safe, and sincere.

Acknowledgement

Acknowledge their complaint and show that you take it seriously.

You may find one or more of the following responses useful:

- I recognise/ acknowledge/ understand that it's hard to speak up

- Thank you for bringing this to me/ telling me about this

- I appreciate you trusting me enough to tell me about this

- This is an important issue for me/ the organisation/ the company

- I will help you to resolve this if I can.

Ensure your conversation takes place in a private area, away from other employees.

Offer them a glass of water to show you care.

You could say, "I know this must be hard for you, so please take your time."

This will be an emotional discussion for your employee. Be prepared for periods of silence or tears as they tell their story.

Listen actively

It's important that your employee feels your only priority is hearing them out.

Make sure you're not distracted or preoccupied with other matters.

Turn off the ringer on your phone.

Show that you are actively listening by using both verbal and non-verbal responses.

Non-verbal responses

- Face your employee and lean forward a little (but not too much or it may be seen as aggressive).

- Adopt an open, warm posture (concerned facial expression, legs and arms uncrossed).

- Maintain soft, warm eye contact.

- Nod your head signaling 'yes, I understand', not necessarily 'I agree'.

Semi-verbal responses

- Make encouraging noises, eg 'mm', 'ah', 'uh-huh'. These all encourage your employee to continue.

Verbal responses

Paraphrase

Repeat back to your employee what you think was said but in your own words.

This will reassure them that you understand – or sometimes that you didn't understand – so they can clarify what they meant.

Reflect feelings

- If you have detected a particular feeling in your employee, reflect it back to them.

- For example, "It sounds like you feel hurt/ angry/ betrayed/ let down/ scared/ vulnerable/ excluded.

- Test if you have properly understood or interpreted their feelings correctly.

- Understanding their feelings shows that you empathise and will often lead to further disclosures.

Record of incidents

Ask the complainant if they have kept a record of the incidents which form the basis of their complaint.

If they haven't, say "Would you be willing to write down what happened?"

Your employee may be wary of 'writing things down', thinking this elevates their complaint to formal.

It's a good idea to say "When you write down what happened, it doesn't make a complaint formal. It just makes it easier to understand and address each allegation you make.

It can still be dealt with informally if that is your preference." (Not in the US as stated in Chapter 6).

If they struggle to write, you should write down what they say. To avoid making your employee uncomfortable about this, you could say:

- "Would it be easier if I write down what you say and type it up later?"

- "Let me read back to you what I wrote so that you can hear your words with my voice. I'm happy to change anything as we go through your story."

Summarise

At the end summarise all that has been said to check if you have the whole picture.

Invite further contributions by asking open questions:

- "Tell me more about…"

- "How did that happen?"

Take your own notes

In addition to your employee's documentation, you should keep your own notes of your conversations. These should be factual and free of your opinion.

Your documentation will be vital if the claim is escalated to formal or legal action.

Reluctant complainant

A common approach from an employee who thinks they're being harassed or bullied is to say to you: "I want to tell you about X, but I don't want you to do anything about it."

Agreeing not to do anything at this stage could put you in an awkward position, especially if they tell you about behaviour that is a criminal offence.

It's a good idea to say: "I will keep what you say confidential unless you tell me something that is a criminal offence." (Incidents that are criminal offences are rare, so don't be too concerned).

There is also the danger that later on your employee could make a formal complaint, saying "I told my manager three months ago and they did nothing about it."

To mitigate this concern, take a few minutes to discuss the options available and steps to follow. Help them understand the full process and the protection the organisation provides.

Challenge the 'worst case scenario' stories

Complainants often build stories in their head about the worst-case scenario before they even approach you.

For example, if they complain they'll:

- be dismissed

- have to resign from their job

- have their performance downgraded

- not be able to get a reference or receive a bad reference.

Remind them that they're a valued employee.

They would never be dismissed, forced to resign or have their performance downgraded for complaining about harassment or bullying, in good faith.

If they leave the job at any time in the future, a complaint will not affect any reference you provide.

All of these actions would fall under the definitions of victimisation or retaliation and are unlawful or illegal.

Reassure them that if they raise their concerns, you'll help them to deal with the situation.

Refusal to take action

After discussing the options, your employee may still not want you to take any action.

 If so, you need to keep a record of this.

After the meeting, write a summary of what was discussed and agreed.

Put this in an email and send it to your employee.

Ask them to respond to your email by return if they disagree with anything in your summary.

On Notice: In the US, employers are 'on notice' and required to take action to prevent recurring behaviour, directed at the original employee (see chapter 6).

This means you must investigate complaints of harassment, even if your employee states they don't want to make a formal complaint or don't want an investigation to occur.

Appendix E at the back of the book explains how to carry out an investigation in the US.

Getting a productive outcome

When your employee seems adamant about you not taking action, you may feel your hands are tied.

However, if they really didn't want you to do anything about their complaint, they wouldn't have said anything at all.

The comment is usually made because they're fearful of the consequences of speaking up.

The fact that they've approached you and said something gives you a lead-in.

When it relates to harassment or bullying, you can reassure them by saying some of the following:

- "I will only pursue your complaint if you agree for me to take it further."

- "Let me explain the different ways the organisation/ I could deal with your complaint."

- "We can resolve your complaint informally or formally, and the choice is yours."

- "After I've explained the process/ different options open to you, you can go away and think about what you would like to do next."

- "I will do everything I can to ensure you are not victimised/ penalised for speaking up."

- "The organisation would discipline any individual who threatened or penalised you for speaking up about harassment or bullying."

It Stops Now!

What <u>not</u> to say or do

Again, your response is critical. You don't want to
sabotage the initial meeting or a legitimate complaint
inadvertently. Let's look at the unhelpful comments or
reactions you want to avoid.

A personal challenge to the alleged recipient

- I think you're being over-sensitive

- I think you've taken what was said/ done the wrong
  way

- I find what you said hard to believe

- You need to learn to take a joke

- Might you have a chip on your shoulder about this?

- Your colleague X is the same race/religion/ has a
  disability/ is gay or lesbian and they're not offended
  by (describe the behaviour).

Taking the side of or defending the alleged
perpetrator

- X wouldn't do that/ say that

- You've misinterpreted what X said

- X is just very direct/ abrupt/ to the point

- X is like that with everyone; it's just the way they
  are, they won't change

- My advice would be to just keep out of X's way

- X brings a lot of sales/ funding/ money/ contracts into this organisation so no-one will challenge his/ her behaviour

- X is highly thought of in this organisation/ by the owner/ senior managers/ board members, so I'd be cautious what you say about him/ her if I were you.

One or two of the comments listed above may be valid and appropriate, once the facts are known, but not as part of the first conversation.

Doing nothing

Failure to act is often more damaging than an inadequate response.

Avoid talking yourself into ignoring the issue by believing or saying:

- These things blow over if you just give them more time

- It sounds like typical workplace banter to me

- If you speak up, you'll be seen as a troublemaker

- If I say anything to X, it will probably make things worse

- It's your word against theirs

- Unless there is independent proof or witnesses, I can't do anything

- These issues are hard to resolve; my advice is not to say anything

- It would be better if you dealt with this yourself without involving management/ human resources/ the trade union

- Leave it with me (and then do nothing about it).

You may feel you're helping by acknowledging how difficult it can be to pursue a complaint.

However, you've only pointed out all the possible negative consequences of speaking out.

This could shut down anyone coming to you in the future.

Consequences of inaction

If you mishandle the initial discussion, it's unlikely they'll take their complaint further. You may be relieved at their decision.

Unfortunately, the issue hasn't gone away.

The alleged harasser or bully has not been challenged about their actions, so their behaviour is likely to continue.

Let's look at what may happen next.

Recipient leaves

Your employee will put up with it for a while longer, and it's likely to affect their work performance negatively.

Eventually, they will take action.

This could be to ask for a transfer to another team, apply for another job internally or externally, or resign because they cannot tolerate the behaviour any longer.

You've lost a good member of staff for all the wrong reasons.

The recipient makes a formal complaint

Alternatively, the inappropriate behaviour continues until the recipient has had enough.

They side-step you and make a formal complaint to the business owner, senior manager, human resources or a Trade Union Representative.

An investigation is carried out.

It's likely the complainant will say you actively discouraged them from taking action when they raised their concerns earlier.

You may be found responsible along with the perpetrator in any investigation.

And if it escalates to legal action, could also be held personally liable.

Intermediate evaluation of the complaint

Once your employee has shared their complaint, you need to do a quick, initial analysis.

Does the claim satisfy the definitions of harassment or bullying? Or does it seem to be a difference of opinion or a misunderstanding?

You may not have enough information to make a clear distinction. That's okay. You can always ask the employee to give you a little time to consider the complaint.

Schedule a follow-up meeting, ideally on the next business day, to discuss the proper response.

If you decide the complaint is harassment or bullying, you should pursue the steps outlined in the next chapters.

If you conclude, their complaint does not fall within the definitions of harassment and bullying, discuss other ways of addressing their concerns.

Chapter 9

The 4-step BIFF process: Teach your staff to deal with incidents

Despite your best efforts to create a respectful culture, incidents may still arise.

You can deal with a large proportion of harassment or bullying allegations or incidents informally if you are made aware in the early stages. Most recipients want:

- the behaviour they are experiencing to stop

- their complaint(s) dealt with in confidence

- only those directly involved to hear about the incident(s)

- to be able to carry on doing their job without further interference or payback.

Most recipients prefer an informal response in the early stages.

The advantage of informal resolution is that you can instigate the methods quickly before the behaviour escalates into a more serious concern.

Using the BIFF feedback process to address complaints

The first option your employee has for dealing with inappropriate behaviour is to challenge the actions they object to themselves.

The alleged perpetrator may be unaware of the effect their behaviour is having on your employee.

If no-one tells them, they're unlikely to change.

The BIFF feedback process is an effective way of confronting inappropriate behaviour face-to-face, or for formulating a response in writing.

You can coach your staff to use the BIFF process to address issues or incidents with colleagues or managers.

This approach works best if you encourage your employee to remain calm and unemotional.

Behaviour (B)

The first stage of the process refers to behaviour. Your employee describes the actions, comments or behaviours they consider unacceptable.

You should emphasise the importance of being specific and not labelling the behaviour.

- **Specific**: "There have been occasions like the one this afternoon and last Tuesday when your voice was raised/ very loud when you spoke to me in front of other staff."

- **Label (to be avoided):** "You're always shouting at me!"

Impact (I)

The second step is for your employee to describe the impact of their colleague's or manager's actions or behaviour.

"I found it difficult to concentrate on what was being said/ difficult to take part in the meeting/ difficult to carry on doing my job, afterwards."

Feelings (F)

The third step is to describe how the behaviour made your employee feel if that is appropriate.

It is vital to use 'I' language, not 'you' language.

- "I felt upset/ undermined/ embarrassed by what you said," not

- "You did that to/ knew that would upset/ undermine/ embarrass me." (Which is accusatory and likely to be denied or challenged).

Your employee explaining how they felt can be very powerful in these conversations.

The perpetrator can say they didn't intend to upset your employee.

But they cannot challenge or deny your employee's reaction or feelings.

Future (F)

The final step is for your employee to describe how they would like the behaviour to be different.

- "In future, I would like/ prefer to hear your feedback/ have problems highlighted in a less public setting/ in a less forceful way/ in a quieter tone."

- Ask for the current behaviour to stop.

The desired outcome at the end of the conversation is that both your employees agree how things will be different in the future and put this into practice.

Offer support

Your employee may be hesitant about having a direct conversation with the perpetrator.

Offer to role-play a conversation with them, using the BIFF process.

You can provide a safe environment for them to practice what to say and to help them anticipate responses.

Chapter 10

The 5-stage ABCDE feedback model for speaking to a bully or harasser

Serious incidents of bullying or harassment generally start with minor incidents.

Failure to take action on your part risks giving the perpetrator a message that their behaviour is OK.

It also creates resentment from any employee who is the recipient of their behaviour. In either circumstance, the situation could escalate.

If you observe inappropriate behaviour or your employee asks you to intervene on their behalf, you should address it as soon as possible.

The ABCDE feedback model

The ABCDE feedback model gives you a framework for:

- preparing your evidence and facts before approaching your employee, who is the alleged perpetrator

- providing feedback to your employee in a five-step sequential order

- making sure any agreed actions and outcomes are completed.

It is based on similar principles to the BIFF process but provides you with steps better aligned with your role as a manager.

The five stages are:

- **A**sk

- **B**ehaviour

- **C**hance to Respond & **C**onsequences

- **D**o

- **E**valuate.

Stage A: Ask

Ask yourself a series of questions before engaging the alleged perpetrator of the behaviour:

'Do I have the facts about the behaviour I am about to address?'

- Make sure you're clear about the behaviours, actions or comments you observed that were inappropriate.

- If an employee approaches you with a complaint, ask them to write down exactly what happened – what was actually said or done by the alleged perpetrator – not a summary.

'What is my desired outcome at the end of this discussion?'

Be clear about your desired outcome before speaking to the alleged perpetrator.

Do you want them to:

- accept that their behaviour was inappropriate?

- apologise to the recipient for their behaviour?

- give an assurance that the behaviour won't happen again?

- or all of these?

Stage B: Behaviour

Describe precisely what you observed.

Alternatively, what your employee reported was said or done by the alleged perpetrator.

Be specific about the behaviour you want to address during your conversation, such as:

- the actual comments or actions witnessed by you, or

- particular comments and/or actions reported to you by the recipient.

As with the BIFF model, be specific and factual. Don't label the behaviour.

"Samir, Alex said you called him 'a total idiot' in front of his colleagues."

Stage C: Chance to respond and Consequences

Chance to respond

At this stage, you should ask Samir to respond to the allegation.

Listen to what he says.

He may immediately take responsibility and apologise, or he may try to defend his actions.

He may also wholly deny the accusation.

Regardless, it's essential to allow him to share his side of the story.

You may be able to prompt a constructive response from him by stating:

"You don't normally shout at colleagues, Samir. What caused you to react like that?"

He may feel less defensive if you acknowledge that the behaviour is out of character.

Consequences

Your next step is to clarify the impact of the behaviour.

"Alex is angry about being called an idiot and for being shouted at in front of his team."

Explaining the consequences of their actions is key to helping someone understand why you are highlighting their behaviour.

117

Stage D: Do

This is where you agree on what your employee will do to address the situation.

"I acknowledge that Alex's mistake caused a lot more work for your team. But it's never acceptable to call a colleague a total idiot. I'd like you to apologise to him and give me your assurance that it won't happen again."

It is essential to agree on a timeframe for this response so you can hold the employee accountable for following up on your discussion.

Be specific, eg:

"I'll follow up with both of you in a couple of days, on Wednesday morning."

Stage E: Evaluate

Assess whether the agreed actions have taken place and/or the situation has been resolved.

Successful outcome

It is important to reinforce positive behaviour change if you want it to continue.

"Thank you for apologising to Alex straight away, and for agreeing not to take your frustration out on others in future."

Unsuccessful outcome

If, on the other hand, your employee

- refuses to apologise

- apologises in an unconvincing or insincere manner

- continues to criticise their colleague to their face or behind their back

…it's vital to address their continuing unacceptable behaviour.

"Samir, I hear you've been telling colleagues that Alex is useless at his job. We discussed this on Monday. It's not acceptable to criticise your colleagues publicly in this way. I have set aside some time this afternoon to discuss this with you fully."

Remember your employee's behaviour may not change after one conversation.

You may need to have further discussions to resolve the matter.

If this doesn't work, you may need to take disciplinary action.

Using the ABCDE model to address a sexual harassment allegation

Sexual harassment complaints are sensitive and require a supportive approach.

Below is an example conversation between a manager and Paul, an employee.

Background

Jo tells you that her colleague Paul 'creeped her out' last night when she was leaving work.

She wants you to do something about it.

Ask

You ask Jo what Paul said and did that made her feel that way.

You ask her what she wants as an outcome.

She wants him to apologise and not make similar comments to her again.

Behaviour

You arrange to speak with Paul and say:

"Paul, I've just had a conversation with Jo. Last night when she was leaving work, she said you stared at her chest and said: 'You ought to wear tight-fitting clothes more often as they show off your figure perfectly'."

Chance to respond

"Do you remember talking to Jo and what you said, Paul?"

Listen to Paul's response. Follow up with any clarifying questions.

Paul says "I was complimenting her. Most women would be flattered by what I said – I can't believe she's complained!"

Consequences

"Jo said she was embarrassed and didn't want to come into work and face you this morning."

Do

Guide Paul on what to do to sort out the situation.

"Comments about a colleague's appearance, especially those that have a sexual implication, are inappropriate. Some women might view your comments as a compliment, Paul, but Jo didn't. She was embarrassed by them. What will you say to her?"

Establish a firm timeline to follow up on any actions agreed.

Evaluate

Successful outcome

"Paul, Jo said you didn't recall staring at her chest, but you apologised for making those comments to her. You also said you wouldn't make comments about her appearance again. She's happy with that. Thank you."

Unsuccessful outcome

"Paul, I've just spoken to Jo. She said you didn't apologise. Instead, you told her she was pathetic and should learn to take a compliment."

"I need to speak with you now about the next steps."

In this instance, you should ensure Paul understands that a formal complaint could follow if the situation cannot be resolved informally.

Using the ABCDE model to address racial harassment

Racial harassment complaints also require a sensitive and supportive approach.

Background

Maja complains about her colleague Sue making racist remarks in the staff canteen. Maja says she was sitting on the next table to Sue at lunch. She heard Sue talking to her colleagues about immigrants.

Ask

You ask Maja to tell you exactly what she heard and who else was present.

You ask her what she wants as an outcome. Maja wants Sue to stop making offensive comments about immigrants and understand how hurtful her comments were.

Behaviour

"Sue, I've just had a conversation with Maja about comments you made in the staff canteen yesterday at around 1 pm. You were sitting with Errol and Claire."

"She heard you say: 'All these immigrants taking our jobs and benefits should go back home to their own countries'."

Chance to respond

Your next step would be to ask for a response from Sue.

"Do you remember making those comments, Sue?"

"I realise that it was a private conversation, but it was overheard. We have staff from many countries working here and you made those comments in a very public space?"

Consequences

"Maja was upset because she's Polish and has only been in this country for five years. She thinks your comments were aimed at her and her family."

Do

Guide Sue on how to address the situation.

"I accept that we all make comments, sometimes without thinking. And your comments were not aimed at Maja or anyone else who works here. However, Maja felt they were directed at her. What will you do to deal with the situation?"

Evaluate

Successful outcome

"Sue, thank you for speaking to Maja and saying your comments were wrong and not targeted at her or her family. She appreciated your apology."

Unsuccessful outcome

"Maja said you're ignoring her and won't speak to her. I am disappointed that you've chosen to react like this. Excluding colleagues is a form of harassment and will be dealt with as a disciplinary matter if we cannot resolve it. Let's sit down now and talk through what you'll do."

Ensure that Sue understands that a formal complaint could follow if the situation cannot be resolved informally.

Using the ABCDE model when the complainant wishes to remain anonymous

Sometimes you receive a complaint, and the employee wants to remain anonymous.

Background

Charles is in his mid-60s. He approaches you because he was upset about a conversation overhead after a meeting.

Gina, a team leader, was complaining about the number of older employees on staff.

125

Ask

Charles tells you he was getting a cup of coffee when he heard Gina and another employee talking. He heard Gina say:

"I'm so tired of explaining our systems to staff. I can't believe how many dense old people we have working here. We need to replace them with some younger staff."

Charles said he was angered by Gina's comment but isn't comfortable speaking to her, as she's in a higher position.

Behaviour

You go and speak with Gina.

"Gina, I've learned that you've made some negative comments about some of our older employees."

Chance to respond

You provide Gina with a chance to respond.

"Does that sound accurate?"

"Yes, some employees are less comfortable working with computers. But no-one masters every system we have immediately."

Consequences

"Our organisation has always benefited from having a wide range of experiences and backgrounds, including years of experience. We should help everyone be successful here, not insult or undermine them because of their age."

Do

Guide Gina on how to handle her frustrations.

"Let me know if you think someone could benefit from additional training. I need everyone to be self-sufficient in using the systems."

Evaluate

Successful outcome

"Gina, I appreciate you acknowledging your frustration and owning your comments. I look forward to working with you to help everyone on the team be successful."

Unsuccessful outcome

"Gina, I saw an email you just sent stating that, 'anyone who doesn't understand how to enter customer changes must be a dinosaur'.

Comments like that are bullying and unacceptable in my team. I'll be following up with you later today to discuss this further."

The alleged perpetrator denies the allegations

In any of these situations, the alleged perpetrator may deny the allegations outright. In these circumstances:

You could ask them why they think the complainant made the allegations if they are untrue.

- Your employee may not see their behaviour as harassment or bullying. You should discuss this with them. Share your observations or perspective where appropriate.

- You may discover there is a history of disagreements between your two employees and the allegations are part of that. You can explore this further with both your employees.

You could explain that the complainant asked for the situation to be resolved informally.

- This means the complainant wants to settle the issue in a conciliatory manner, which is the reason for your approach.

- Let your employee know that formal action may be the next step if the situation cannot be resolved informally.

- Allow them time to think this through.

If your employee continues to deny the allegations, make sure you keep a written record of your discussion.

- Your notes should summarise the complaint and what you did to try and resolve the situation.

- If there are further allegations against the same employee in the future, your notes will help decide what action to take.

- Your notes will also form part of the investigation if the complaint escalates to formal action.

Appendix E Summary of US and UK investigation processes explains how to carry out a formal investigation

Chapter 11

Addressing exclusion: Interventions that work

Exclusion of one of your employees by other team members is a common form of harassment or bullying in the workplace.

It is also very damaging.

Employees who experience prolonged exclusion eventually leave their jobs, usually with their confidence undermined.

Employees targeted by exclusion rarely complain about it because the behaviour is passive and based on the absence of action. For example, "My colleagues leave me out of conversations."

You may notice it long before the employee makes a complaint.

If your staff member does raise it, you'll usually hit a brick wall when you approach the alleged perpetrator(s) directly with their complaint.

Their reaction is usually one or more of the following:

- "I haven't said or done anything to X"

- "I have nothing in common with X"

- "You can't make people be friends with each other"

- "X doesn't try to fit in with us"

- "X is the problem, not me – he/she is stand-offish/ aloof/ unfriendly."

These reactions make it hard for you to deal with the behaviour. You're stuck trying to prove that something didn't happen.

When the exclusion was intentional, the perpetrators win. Without a consequence, they will feel confident in doing it again.

Fortunately, there are numerous ways of addressing exclusion in a team.

I am going to use a real workplace situation to illustrate the actions you could take.

Background

Sara joined a well-established team of eight people, in an administrative role, ten weeks ago. Her manager is Lloyd.

Sara is 25. She is a devout Christian and spends much of her free time at her church and sings in the choir.

She does not drink alcohol and will not go to venues that sell alcohol.

She does not watch much TV and does not engage in social media.

Her work colleagues, who are also in their 20s, regularly go to a local bar after work and communicate with each other via social media.

They watch the same programmes on TV and have a lot in common.

The team is multi-racial. Three employees have a common heritage, and their first language is not English.

From the outset, they considered Sara to be different and 'odd'.

As the weeks have gone by, they have engaged with her less and less and now ignore her completely.

Lloyd's observations

Lloyd observed the team leaving Sara out of conversations. He noted them going on breaks and to lunch without Sara.

If Sara sat at a table first in the staff cafe, the rest of the team would sit elsewhere. If Sara sat with the team, they would either finish their food and drinks quickly or talk over Sara as if she wasn't there.

Lloyd was uncomfortable about what he was seeing.

Taking action

His first response was to speak to Sara one-to-one in private. He asked her how she was getting on with the rest of the team.

She quickly became tearful. She said she enjoyed the work but didn't feel she fitted in with the rest of her colleagues. Colleagues 'blanked her' and avoided speaking to her unless they had to.

She said she was looking for another job.

Lloyd was alarmed by her comments.

In his view, Sara was a very able and competent member of staff whom he did not want to lose from his team.

What did Lloyd do to address the situation?

His first step was to offer Sara his support.

He said he'd observed team members ignoring her.

He explained that exclusion is a form of harassment and bullying. It was not acceptable in his team, and he would be dealing with it.

Lloyd has options at this point.

He could ask Sara what she wants to do or what she would like him to do. She may have some ideas.

However, he needs to be careful with this question. Sara is likely to respond by saying, "Nothing."

If Lloyd respects her request and does nothing to improve her experience, Sara will almost certainly leave the organisation.

A better approach is to take control of the situation by 'owning the problem'.

This was Lloyd's preference. He reassured Sara that he would not say she had made a complaint.

He would tackle the team's behaviour from his perspective, saying he considered their behaviour to be unacceptable.

He explained that he would meet with each team member individually to share his observations and set out his expectations.

Sara was happy with the approach Lloyd suggested.

As a manager, you are responsible for setting the standards of appropriate behaviour in your team.

You are entitled to address instances of unacceptable behaviour observed within your team.

Lloyd followed the ABCDE Feedback Model when addressing his team's behaviour.

Ask

Lloyd gathered his facts by observing his team's behaviour around Sara.

He made a note of the actions of each team member which he considered to be examples of exclusion or other inappropriate behaviour.

He was clear about his outcome before he approached his team members.

He wanted each member of the team to:

- stop ignoring Sara in the office
- engage with her, beyond yes and no answers
- say good morning to her when she came into work as they did with others
- stop leaving her on her own or talking across her at breaks and lunch.

Behaviour

Lloyd spoke to each member of the team, one-to-one, focusing on the behaviours he'd observed, such as:

- "When Sara said 'Good Morning' to you yesterday, and today, you didn't respond even though she was standing right next to you."

- "When Sara went to sit with you and your colleague at the coffee break, I noticed neither of you spoke to her the whole time she was with you."

- "When you and your colleagues X and Y went to lunch today, Sara was already there, but you went and sat at the other side of the restroom/café."

- "When Sara asked you a question about a file she was trying to locate, your answers to her questions were very abrupt and in my view, unhelpful."

- "I have observed you and your two colleagues speaking in your own language when Sara is working with you, which excludes her."

Chance to respond

Lloyd asked each team member for their response using similar questions to these:

- "How come you never answer Sara when she says, 'Good Morning' to you?"

- "Why do you ignore Sara when she sits with you at break?"

- "What's your reason for being so abrupt with Sara, when she asks you questions about work matters?"

- "How would you feel if you were treated in that way by your colleagues?"

137

Be mindful that not everyone will own up to their behaviour.

Referencing your observations can encourage some ownership.

Consequences

Lloyd stated the consequences of their behaviour to each team member, as follows:

- "Ignoring a colleague who greets you in the morning is disrespectful in my view."

- "Leaving Sara on her own in the café at breaks is inappropriate, from my perspective."

- "Giving abrupt yes and no questions when a colleague asks you a question is unhelpful in my team."

- "Speaking in your own language when working with a colleague who does not understand what you're saying, is not appropriate within this organisation."

Appeal to your staff members' sense of decency

If a direct approach with Lloyd's team isn't feasible, he could appeal to their sense of decency instead.

With Sara's permission this would involve, for example:

- telling each employee, "Sara was in tears this morning because she feels excluded"

- explaining that Sara is looking for another job as she thinks no-one wants her in the team.

Your staff are probably reasonable people.

When they realise their actions have led to Sara feeling like this, they may be horrified.

This alone may be enough for them to start including her.

If there is a ringleader

Through your observations and discussions with staff members, you may discover a 'ringleader'.

Often one person, with influence within the team, is instigating this behaviour.

If that is the case, you should concentrate on tackling that person's behaviour first.

Do

Lloyd's next step was to ascertain what each staff member would do to address the situation, and how their behaviour towards Sara would change.

He used similar questions to these:

- "How will your behaviour towards Sara change?"

- "What assurance can you give me that your behaviour towards Sara will be different from now on?"

- "What will you do to help Sara feel more included?"

- "How can you help me to integrate Sara into the team?"

- "Have you agreed you'll communicate in English in future when Sara is present?"

Re-engage the group

Let's look at additional steps that you can take to re-engage your team after your one-to-one conversations. Lloyd used a number of these.

Also, if direct one-to-one conversations with your staff aren't realistic, you can use these techniques instead.

Choose the method(s) that would work best in your workplace culture.

Provide a buddy

Ask a staff member to act as a 'buddy' to befriend the excluded staff member and help you integrate them back into the team.

You can ask this employee to share their observations of Sara, in this instance, and talk through some ideas to help bring her back into the team.

Break up the clique or gang

You can break up the dynamics of the clique by creating situations that limit opportunities to exclude one staff member, such as:

- getting your staff to work in pairs

- asking small groups of staff to work on projects together

- rotating jobs between your staff members, so they get used to working with different people

- staggering or reallocating breaks, so staff interact with various team members

- moving staff members who are instigators of the behaviour into other work areas.

You might think that moving the person who is being excluded is an easier option. Only do this as a last resort.

Legally this would be viewed as victimisation or retaliation because they are being penalised twice. Once due to the behaviour of the team; the second time by being moved to a different work area.

It's also a successful outcome for the perpetrators who wanted to get rid of their colleague. This will encourage them to repeat it with other employees.

Training or briefings

It would be useful to run an interactive training or briefing session with your staff on:

- harassment and bullying or treating colleagues with dignity and respect

- your organisation's values which would include:
  - o the behaviours and actions which illustrate the values
  - o the practices and activities that do not represent the values.

Other options

Lead on a project

If your excluded staff member has particular expertise or competence in an area, you could ask them to lead on a project that is important to the whole team.

Organise a social or team building event

Organise an event inside or outside of work to give everyone a chance to get to know each other in a different setting.

Choose a location and activities that are appropriate for all employees.

Evaluate

The final stage was for Lloyd to evaluate what happened after his interventions.

He spoke to Sara to find out how she was feeling and whether the situation had improved.

Then he observed the team's interactions to see if they were engaging with Sara.

He also spoke to individual team members to assess their views.

Successful outcome

Lloyd acknowledged and reinforced the actions of staff members who changed their behaviour towards Sara.

"I appreciate the efforts you've made to include Sara, thank you", or "Sara seems much happier now, thanks to you."

You should always give feedback on positive outcomes if you want them to continue.

Unsuccessful outcome

Where the behaviour of individual staff members had not changed, Lloyd repeated the actions above or implemented options he had not tried.

His interventions worked.

Sara has stayed in her job. She has friends on the team and is happy coming to work now.

If these actions do not resolve the situation in your workplace, you should make it clear to each staff member that the current situation is not acceptable.

Exclusion and ignoring a colleague are forms of harassment or bullying.

If you have exhausted all informal solutions, the remaining option would be to take disciplinary action.

Your observations of the inappropriate behaviours carried out by your staff member(s) would be the evidence.

Chapter 12

Informal resolution: Mediation, facilitated meetings and informal discussions

Other proven, informal methods to resolve allegations or incidents are:

- Mediation
- Facilitated meetings
- Informal discussions.

Mediation

Mediation requires a professional mediator to take a 'no-blame approach' to resolve issues in your employees' relationship.

The goal isn't to prove that one person is right, and the other is wrong.

Both parties are encouraged to recognise and accept that their relationship is not working.

145

The process aims to help both employees find a different, constructive way of working together in the future.

Many external trained mediators provide this service if you do not have a trained mediator on staff.

Facilitated meeting

Alternatively, you could facilitate a meeting between your employees adopting the techniques used in mediation.

It's essential that you make the no-blame purpose of the meeting clear to both employees at the outset.

Explain that you aim to help them to:

- understand each other's perspective of the issues not working in their relationship, and

- find ways of interacting effectively with each other in future.

As the facilitator, you would ask relevant questions of each employee to explore what has happened and why it caused them difficulties.

You would follow up with questions to find out what would work better for them in the future.

The questions you might ask include:

Person A

- "What happened, eg, shouting, ignoring, undermining?"

- "How did it affect you?"

- "What would you see as a different or better way of dealing with such situations in the future?"
  - "What could you do?"
  - "What do you want B to do?"
  - "Please say more than 'Not shout at me anymore'."

Person B

- "What actions or behaviours do you think A may have interpreted as bullying?"

147

  o   "What was your intention in those behaviours?"

- "What would you see as a different or better way of dealing with such situations in the future?"

  o   "What could you do?"

  o   "What do you want A to do?"

  o   "Please be as specific as you can."

Any agreed actions would be put in place, with your support where needed.

Ideally, you would do this with both employees present so each person can hear first-hand what the other person says.

If either employee is reluctant, or you feel uncomfortable facilitating the meeting, you can do the exploration with each person separately.

You would bring them back together afterwards to discuss options for moving forward.

Each employee must volunteer to participate in mediation or a facilitated meeting. If they feel they have no choice in the matter, they won't engage with the process.

You'll find a Facilitated meeting – detailed questions template in Appendix D. It includes examples of how it can be used.

Informal resolution of the allegations

Another informal option is for you to speak with the alleged perpetrator on the complainant's behalf.

Your employee may choose this option in preference to participating in a formal complaint process.

If your employee chooses this option, the steps are:

Preparation

• Ask the complainant to provide you with a full written record of the incidents, including dates.

• Meet with them and go through the incidents, clarifying anything unclear in their account.

• Ask the complainant what they want as an outcome, for example:

  o a recognition that their colleague's behaviour was inappropriate

  o an apology

  o an agreement for it not to happen again

  o all of the above, or

  o something else.

Inform the alleged perpetrator

- Arrange a meeting with the alleged perpetrator.

- Let them know that it is to discuss a complaint of harassment and bullying which the complainant wants to resolve informally.

- Inform them that it is an informal discussion so is not part of the disciplinary procedure.

Explain the purpose of the meeting at the outset

- At the start of the meeting, explain that:

  o an allegation of bullying or harassment has been made by X

  o X would prefer to resolve the matter informally asking you (their manager) to raise it on their behalf

  o if you can agree on a satisfactory solution to X's concerns, this will be the end of the matter

  o if it cannot be resolved at this stage, then a formal complaint with a full investigation may be the next step.

- Although the meeting is informal, you must let your employee know that you will:

  o be taking notes

  o keep a record of the discussion as evidence of an informal intervention

○ provide them with a copy of the meeting notes for their approval.

Conduct the meeting

• Go through the complainant's record of the incidents asking for the perpetrator's response.

Successful outcome

• If the perpetrator takes responsibility for the behaviour and/ or agrees to an outcome that is satisfactory to you and the complainant:

○ thank them for their response and/ or agreement

○ write up the notes you took at the meeting and send them a copy for their approval

○ feedback the outcome of the informal approach to the complainant and make a note of their response

○ agree to review the situation regularly.

Unsuccessful outcome

• If the perpetrator denies responsibility for the behaviour alleged by the complainant or makes counter-allegations, you will need to terminate the informal meeting.

• Explain that you will feed their response back to the complainant.

• You will let them know if the complainant decides to make a formal complaint.

- Send them the notes of the meeting for their approval.

Complainant and alleged perpetrator in different teams

The complainant and alleged perpetrator involved in an incident may work in different teams or departments and have different managers.

In these circumstances, you could discuss the best way to resolve the situation with the other person's manager.

If your employee is the complainant, you would need to obtain their agreement before pursuing this option.

If they are open to this option, you would follow the steps outlined in the informal resolution method.

Instead of speaking to the perpetrator directly, you would discuss it with their manager first.

The alleged perpetrator's manager would carry out the informal discussion with their employee.

At the end of the process, you and the other manager would discuss the best way forward. Either with or without the complainant and alleged perpetrator being present.

All four would participate in the solution.

Chapter 13

Why employees might harass or bully others: Causes and solutions

You may assume that harassment or bullying is perpetrated by individuals with malice and an intent to hurt the recipient. This is true of some harassers or bullies, but not the majority.

There are many reasons why one of your managers or staff members might harass or bully another employee. Some of the most common causes and possible solutions are outlined below:

1. They don't realise they're causing offence or upset

Some of your employees won't understand the impact of their behaviour on others. They think their colleagues welcome their comments, humour, intrusive questions, constant inappropriate chatter or practical jokes.

Possible solutions: Make a note of the behaviours you've observed and consider to be inappropriate.

Own the problem yourself and address it immediately, one-to-one. Use the ABCDE Feedback Model described in Chapter 10 to structure your conversation.

2. They feel insecure

When there is uncertainty in your workplace, harassment or bullying incidents tend to increase. This could be due to rumours of redundancies, layoffs or buyouts. Employees fear losing their job, their livelihood and the implications for their career or family. In these circumstances, they are more likely to 'lash out' at their colleagues who may be seen as 'rivals' for their job.

Possible solutions: Explain what is really going on (or share as much as you know) and dispel or minimise the rumours. Challenge any inappropriate behaviour you observe using the ABCDE Feedback Model outlined in Chapter 10.

3. They are jealous or feel threatened by a colleague

Your employee may believe a colleague is more popular, or highly thought of by you, other managers, or team members. They see that colleague as a 'threat' and attempt to undermine them with sarcastic comments, put-downs, spreading malicious gossip or rumours, or in some cases, sabotaging their work.

Possible solutions: Speak to the disgruntled employee one-to-one about how they are performing in their role. Praise them for what they do well. Coach them in areas they could improve. Challenge any inappropriate behaviour you're made aware of, or observe, using the ABCDE Feedback Model outlined in Chapter 10.

4. Pressure of work

At times there are deadlines to meet and not enough hours in the day to achieve them. Your employees feel pressured. They may become curt or abrupt with colleagues. The additional stress and ensuing bad behaviour damages employee morale, resulting in staff complaints.

Possible solutions: Plan ahead for times when you know the workload will be higher. Encourage staff to talk to you if they feel they cannot cope with the workload. Pay special attention to employees' attitudes and tones.

Address instances of disrespectful behaviour immediately, to stop them from escalating. If the situation occurs regularly, consider longer-term solutions.

5. Employees don't like each other or have prejudices against colleagues

Some of your staff may dislike a colleague or have prejudices. They are unlikely to admit this to you. Even if they do, their admission isn't a valid excuse for disrespectful behaviour.

Possible solutions: Remind them that they were employed to do a job and need to be professional with colleagues. State what behaviours you expect them to exhibit when working with their colleague(s) and hold them accountable. Challenge any inappropriate behaviour you observe using the ABCDE Feedback Model outlined in Chapter 10.

6. Personal problems outside of work

Employees are advised 'not to bring their personal problems to work'. However, some of your staff will find it hard to concentrate on their job when there are significant problems in their home life.

Employees may appear distracted and make mistakes or miss deadlines. You might witness emotional outbursts, including bursting into tears or anger, leading to complaints.

Possible solutions: If you notice worrying changes in one of your employee's behaviour, arrange a one-to-one meeting with them. Offer your support if they want to talk about anything.

If they don't want to talk to you, let them know who else they could speak to within the organisation. Tell them about any additional services that your organisation offers to support employees. If they do 'open up to you', offer time off or flexible hours while they deal with any issues in their home life.

7. They are ill

If one of your employees becomes ill with, for example, a mental health condition, it could cause changes to behaviour which are 'out of character' for that individual.

Possible solutions: Follow the steps outlined in the personal problems example above. Offer your support and encourage them to speak with your occupational health service if you think it would help.

If they don't want to go to occupational health or other support services? Seek additional advice on what you should do, from the business owner, senior managers or human resources, if you have them.

Be mindful of the different laws that protect employees from health-related discrimination. You cannot force your staff to take action.

However, you can create a supportive work environment, where they are more likely to ask for help.

8. New staff complain of not feeling part of the team

There is likely to be some exclusion taking place, which is probably inadvertent.

Current employees have already formed friendships.

They are more likely to chat with these colleagues and go on breaks or to lunch with them.

Possible solutions

- Revise your induction process.

- Alternatively, put an induction process in place if you don't have one for new employees joining your team.

- Inform your team about the arrival of a new colleague beforehand. Let them know the date the person is joining and their job role.

- Give the team some background information about the person (with their permission). This will help their colleagues instigate conversations when they start.

- On their first day, ensure you or someone else is there to greet them.

- Introduce them to everyone on the team.

- Allocate a member of the team to be their 'buddy' for the first week to show them around.
  - The buddy makes sure they have someone to go to breaks or lunch with and helps them to get to know other team members.

Chapter 14

Creating a respectful culture: Manager actions

Are you a good role model?

Whether you accept it or not, your staff will look to you as the 'role model' of what is appropriate behaviour in the team. Your actions day-to-day will be closely watched by your staff and will influence their behaviour. Be a good role model of respectful behaviour at all times.

Conscious observer

You have the right to set the behavioural standards in your team. You do not have to wait for a complaint of harassment or bullying before you take action.

Be consciously observant of the behaviour of your team members. Deal with minor incidents immediately to stop inappropriate behaviours from building up.

Early intervention can minimise the likelihood of harassment or bullying incidents from occurring in the team. Also, where an event has occurred, your actions will influence whether it escalates or not.

Example conversation

You: "Tom, I have noticed you mimicking Mary's accent in meetings and talking over her when you disagree with her opinions."

Tom: "Huh, has she been complaining about me – she's got a nerve going to you!"

You: "No, Mary hasn't complained to me. I consider your behaviour to be disrespectful and inappropriate and want it to stop."

Be an active bystander

Active bystanders are people who witness an inappropriate situation unfolding and take steps to intervene and stop the behaviour.

Assume the role of 'active bystander', and you will contribute to a workplace culture where everyone feels respected and included.

It will also prevent inappropriate behaviour from becoming the norm in your team or department.

Active bystander interventions

Active bystander intervention methods have been effective in many workplace settings. Examples of interventions include:

Interrupt the behaviour

When you realise inappropriate behaviour is occurring, find a reason to pull the recipient or perpetrator aside. Or change the conversation to a different topic to distract the person.

Affirm and support the recipient

When someone demeans a colleague or puts their work down, you interject and make clear that criticism shouldn't occur in a public forum. Close by highlighting your team member's positive contributions.

Use humour to call out behaviour

If you notice a colleague engaging in sexually suggestive comments toward another employee, you could interject with a response that makes the point in a light-hearted way, for example, "Hey, remember we're still at work, not in a bar."

Be careful when using humour as the person may misinterpret it as reinforcement of their behaviour. It must carry an unambiguous message of disapproval.

Consider carrying out separate follow up conversations with both employees to reiterate your stance.

De-escalate and calm the perpetrator if other interventions fail

The person exhibiting inappropriate behaviour may become defensive in response to an intervention method.

You can calm the situation by appealing to their principles, or referring to the positive aspects of their character. For example,

"This isn't like you; you're one of the most supportive/ reasonable people I know."

Let other bystanders know they are supported

Be prepared to support other bystanders who attempt to intervene. Say something to the perpetrator, which supports the bystander's intervention, if their initial action failed to solve the problem.

"Jade, I agree with Sam; your comment was inappropriate."

Interventions after the event

If you are uncomfortable or unable to intervene at that moment, speak to the person after the event.

You may need to follow up with everyone who witnessed the interaction. This enables you to demonstrate support and ensure staff know you'll hold employees accountable.

Post-event support

When the interven-
tion is over, offer
your support and
validation to the
person who experi-
enced the inappro-
priate comment or
behaviour. For ex-
ample, "Are you OK?
I saw what hap-
pened. That was
inappropriate."

Commit to or offer to
address the issue
with the perpetrator.

Offer to accompany and support the recipient

You could:

- offer to accompany and support the targeted employee (eg as a witness) if they want to make a complaint

- assist them in speaking to the perpetrator after the event, if that's what they want to do

- inform the recipient that you'll talk to the perpetrator as you also found their behaviour unacceptable.

Talk to the perpetrator in private

If you are their manager, speak to the perpetrator after the event.

Take on the responsibility yourself, for example:

- "I observed you speaking to X with a raised voice this morning in front of other staff. I felt this was an inappropriate way to talk to X, and I could see they were upset/ embarrassed by the situation."

Ask your employee what they will do to address or resolve the situation.

Follow up to check if the agreed actions took place.

Formal complaint

COMPLAINT PROCEDURE

This toolkit has been written to address harassment and bullying in your workplace as early as possible. It's always better to avoid formal action by your interventions if you can.

However, that is not always possible.

Your employee has the right to make a formal complaint if that is their preference.

In those circumstances, you must follow the steps outlined in your organisation's harassment and bullying or grievance procedures.

If you want to see the steps involved in a typical formal investigation in the US and UK, please refer to Appendix E Summary of US and UK investigation processes, at the back of the book.

Next Steps

Thank you from the bottom of my heart for buying my book. I hope you have found the advice and guidance helpful.

I have put everything I know and learned in the last 25 years into this book because I have a passion for supporting business owners and managers who want to do the best for their employees.

If you would like support in implementing the advice, techniques and strategies, please contact me.

Workshops for Managers: My company runs face-to-face and virtual workshops using actor-coaches which teach your managers exactly how to implement everything outlined in this book.

Online Courses: I have also produced a Dealing with Harassment and Bullying online course for staff and managers.

My contact details are:

Email: josiehastings@gmail.com

Phone: +44 1922 643330

Mobile: +44 7957 870294

Website: www.josiehastings.co.uk

Facebook: JHA Online

I look forward to hearing from you!

Courses for Managers

If you want to train your managers or staff to implement the techniques outlined in this book, we can help.

My company can run a bespoke **face-to-face** or **virtual workshop** for you on managing or dealing with harassment and bullying at work. We run workshops for both managers and staff, using actors who are also professional coaches.

We use a variety of techniques to involve participants which creates an engaging and memorable experience.

Attendees on our workshops in the morning can put what they've learned into practice in the afternoon.

Our virtual workshops are run interactively on Zoom or MS Teams with the actor-coaches. We offer 'virtually' the same experience as a face-to-face workshop event.

Coaching practise

We can also provide focused 1:1 coaching with managers as part of a workshop, or after a workshop. Both face-to-face and Zoom or Teams formats work equally well.

The actor-coaches give managers space to practise the skills they need to manage situations with their staff.

They give detailed feedback on body language, voice tone, choice of words and so on, which leads to many light-bulb moments for participants.

Appendices

Appendix A: Laws on harassment and bullying in the UK, ROI, Australia, NZ, Canada and the US

Although the terms harassment and bullying are used interchangeably in the workplace, there are clear legal differences between them.

This becomes significant when one of your employees takes legal action against your organisation.

Harassment

The legal definitions of harassment across the six countries of the United Kingdom (UK), Republic of Ireland (ROI), Australia, New Zealand (NZ), Canada and the United States (US), are similar.

United Kingdom UK (Equality Act 2010)

'Unwanted conduct that has the purpose or effect of either violating another person's dignity or creating an intimidating, hostile, degrading, humiliating or offensive environment for that person.'

There must be a link to the employee's protected characteristic which, in the UK, are: age, disability, gender reassignment; race, religion and belief, sex, or sexual orientation.

Marriage and civil partnership and pregnancy and maternity, which are also protected characteristics, are not included. Harassment on these grounds would fall under one of the other protected characteristics.

Republic of Ireland ROI (Employment Equality Acts 1998-2015)

'Any form of unwanted conduct, related to any of the protected grounds, which has the purpose or effect of violating a person's dignity and creating an intimidating, hostile, degrading, humiliating or offensive environment for the person.'

The protected grounds are age, civil status, disability, family/carer status, gender (including transgender), race, religion, sexual orientation and traveller community membership.

Australia (Fair Work Amendment Act 2013)

'Unwelcome behaviour that offends humiliates or intimidates a person.'

Generally, it is unlawful under federal and, or, state anti-discrimination law if the treatment is based on the person's age, disability, family/carer responsibilities, gender identity, marital status, pregnancy, race, religion or sexual orientation.

New Zealand NZ (Employment Relations Act ERA 2000 and Human Rights Act HRA 1993)

The ERA and HRA protects employees only from sexual and racial harassment.

Sexual Harassment: Behaviour of a sexual nature that is unwelcome or offensive to the recipient.

Racial Harassment: Behaviour that expresses hostility, brings the recipient into contempt or ridicule, or is hurtful or offensive, because of their race, colour, ethnic or national origins.

In both circumstances, the behaviour must be so significant or repeated that it has a negative effect on the recipient's employment, job performance or job satisfaction.

Discrimination: Under both Acts, it is illegal to treat employees unfairly or less favourably than others, on the grounds of their age, disability, employment status, family status, marital status, political opinion, religious or ethical belief, race, sex and sexual orientation.

Canada (Policy on Harassment and Prevention Resolution)

'Improper conduct by an individual that is directed at and offensive to, another individual in the workplace. This includes at any event or any location related to work, and that the individual knew, or ought reasonably to have known, would cause offence or harm.'

Harassment is also included under the Canadian Human Rights Act when it is based on age, disability, family status, gender identity, genetic characteristics, marital status, race, religion, sex, sexual orientation and conviction for a pardoned or suspended offence.

On notice

In Canada, you are 'on notice' which requires you to respond swiftly and carry out investigations into any harassment claims.

However, you are also expected to offer complainants the option of an informal resolution process.

This allows the complainant to attempt to address the behaviour informally before submitting a formal complaint.

Your employee has the option to skip or halt the informal resolution process and move to a formal complaint at any point.

United States US (Title VII Civil Rights Act 1964)

'Unwelcome conduct that is a condition of continued employment or that creates an intimidating, hostile, or offensive work environment.'

The most prominent federal anti-discrimination law in the US is Title VII of the Civil Rights Act of 1964.

The US has separate laws prohibiting discrimination on the grounds of age and disability.

Harassment is a form of discrimination within these laws.

It is illegal when an employee is mistreated because they are a member of a protected class, which are age, disability, race, colour, ethnicity, religion, sex* and national origin.

Also, many US states, including Minnesota and California, have their own anti-discrimination laws expanding protection for employees based upon sexual orientation and/or gender identity.

Federal harassment laws only cover US employers with 15 or more employees. At least half of US states also have sexual harassment laws that cover employers with fewer than 15 employees. As state and local laws vary, you should verify your compliance requirements with local government agencies.

Further complicating compliance is that fact that recent US case law has tended to interpret the protective class of 'sex' in a broader sense, including sexual orientation and gender identity.

Presidential executive orders in recent administrations have both included and excluded this broader interpretation. However, the Act has not been amended to include or address these additional protected classes.

On notice

When an employee brings up a harassment complaint, in the US, you and your employer, are considered to be 'on notice.' You must respond immediately and escalate the complaint to the appropriate person in your organisation to carry out an investigation. Appendix E explains how to carry out an investigation in the US.

Bullying definitions

Laws in the UK, ROI, NZ, Canada and the US prohibit bullying, as with harassment, only when it's linked to an employee's protected characteristic.

Australia applies a broader standard.

Australia (Fair Work Amendment Act 2013)

In Australia, the Fair Work Amendment Act 2013 defines bullying as:

'Repeated unreasonable behaviour by an individual towards a worker which creates a risk to health and safety.

'Bullying is when people repeatedly and intentionally use words or actions against someone or a group of people to cause distress and risk to their well-being.'

Employees don't have to link the behaviour to their protected characteristic to make a legal claim, as is required in other countries.

United Kingdom (ACAS Code of Practice)

In the UK, there are no laws prohibiting bullying, specifically. Instead, employers are expected to implement the guidance in the ACAS Code of Practice which defines bullying as:

'Offensive, intimidating, malicious or insulting behaviour which intentionally or unintentionally undermines, humiliates, denigrates or injures the recipient.'

Bullying is legally different from harassment because it is not connected to the person's protected characteristic.

Bullying may be by an individual or a group of people against an individual or groups of people. It may be obvious, or it may be covert and, as with harassment, does not need to be deliberate to be viewed as unacceptable.

Under the **Health and Safety at Work Act 1974** and **Management of Health and Safety at Work Regulations 1999**, all employers must provide a safe and healthy working environment.

As an employer, you are required to:

• Assess the nature and scale of workplace risks to health and safety. This includes the mental health of your staff.

  o   Harassment or bullying will affect an employee's mental health.

- Ensure there are proper control measures in place to avoid these risks wherever possible.

- Reduce them so far as is reasonably practicable, where not.

Republic of Ireland (Labour Relations Commission Code of Practice 2001)

In the Republic of Ireland (ROI), the Code of Practice produced by the Labour Relations Committee (LRC) defines workplace bullying as:

'Repeated inappropriate behaviour, direct or indirect, whether verbal, physical or otherwise, conducted by one or more persons against another or others, at the place of work and, or in the course of employment, which could reasonably be regarded as undermining the individual's right to dignity at work.

An isolated incident of the behaviour described in this definition may be an affront to dignity at work but, as a once-off incident, is not considered to be bullying.'

In the ROI, **Section 8 of the Safety, Health and Welfare at Work Act 2005** states that:

'Employers are required to prevent any improper conduct or behaviour likely to put the safety, health and welfare of employees at risk.'

New Zealand (WorkSafe)

Legislation in New Zealand does not prohibit workplace bullying explicitly. WorkSafe (the health and safety regulator) defines workplace bullying as:

'Repeated and unreasonable behaviour directed towards a worker or group of workers that can lead to physical or psychological harm'.

The Employment Relations Act 2000 (ERA) outlines penalties for certain breaches of the duty of good faith within an employment relationship. Repeated verbal or emotional attacks on an employee may breach this duty.

Health and Safety at Work Act 2015 (HSWA) Employers must ensure, so far as is reasonably practicable, the health and safety of workers which includes minimising the likelihood of bullying by putting in control measures.

Harmful Digital Communications Act 2015 (HDCA) This Act aims to deter, prevent and mitigate the harm caused to individuals by digital communications. Harm means serious emotional distress.

The Act covers any form of electronic communication including emails, texts, websites, blogs, online forums, social media sites or phone apps.

Canada (Canadian Centre for Occupational Health and Safety CCOHS)

Few Canadian jurisdictions have legislation which relates explicitly to bullying. Although some jurisdictions include bullying under the term 'hostile work environment'.

The Canadian Centre for Occupational Health and Safety (CCOHS) defines workplace bullying as:

'Acts or verbal comments that could mentally hurt or isolate a person in the workplace. Sometimes, bullying can involve negative physical contact as well.

Bullying usually involves repeated incidents or a pattern of behaviour that is intended to intimidate, offend, degrade or humiliate a particular person or group of people.'

United States

Neither federal law nor the law of any state prohibits workplace bullying outright. It is illegal only when it violates laws prohibiting discrimination and harassment in the workplace (as outlined above).

Although some states in the US include bullying under the term, 'hostile work environment.'

The Workplace Bullying Institute (WBI) in the US defines bullying as:

'Repeated, health-harming mistreatment of one or more persons (the targets) by one or more perpetrators. It is abusive conduct that is threatening, humiliating, or intimidating, or work interference or sabotage, which prevents work from getting done, or verbal abuse.'

Employer liability

In the US, federal law and some state laws can hold you, as the employer, liable for harassment by supervisors, high-level managerial employees, or officers. This is regardless of whether or not you knew about the harassment.

The definition of supervisor differs from state to state. In some states, you would be viewed as a supervisor if you had the authority to transfer, suspend, promote, demote, assign duties or impose discipline.

In other states recommending such actions to the decision-maker, would be sufficient.

In practice, this means your company might not be liable for a particular employee's actions under federal law, but still be liable under your state's laws.

As the employer, you are expected to follow the rules that are more favourable to your employee. Your employee is also entitled to make claims under both federal and state laws at the same time.

Individual employee liability

Under the laws of some states (but not federal law), individual employees who engage in harassment and bullying may be held personally liable.

If based in these states, you should remind employees they can be sued for harassment or bullying of their co-workers.

Their personal assets would be at stake in any lawsuit.

Protection for nonemployees

Many states extend protection against harassment beyond employees to include other individuals you may engage, such as independent contractors.

Training supervisors

Providing anti-harassment training for your supervisors is obligatory in some states. Connecticut and Maine specify the provision of sexual harassment training.

California requires such training to cover all protected groups and to include the prevention of abusive conduct in general.

Training is not a mandatory requirement in other states but is strongly recommended.

Definitions of victimisation or retaliation

Countries with anti-discrimination legislation also prohibit victimisation (UK, ROI, Australia and NZ) or retaliation (the US and Canada).

These terms have a specific meaning in this legislation. They are defined similarly in each country as taking action to penalise an employee who, in good faith, has:

- made allegations or complaints of harassment or bullying, or

- helped other employees who are making a complaint, by providing evidence, or acting as a witness.

Examples include:

- dismissal, failure to renew a contract or demotion

- refusing training or development opportunities without good reason

- blocking promotion or a transfer to another job, without cause

- changing pay or bonus payments

- varying hours or shifts, making it difficult for the employee to continue to work

- changing the type of work given to the employee, eg overloading them with work or giving them only tedious or menial tasks to carry out.

Appendix B: Micro-aggressions

Towards employees from minority ethnic groups

- Q: Where are you from? A: London. Q: But where are you really from?

- When was the last time you went 'home'?

- Can I touch your hair?

- It's hard to pronounce your name, so we'll call you Sue/Sam.

- Does your family know you have a white boyfriend/girlfriend?

- What does your partner's family think about him/her being with you?

- All Asians want to be doctors, dentists, accountants or lawyers; they don't want to work in xx.

- Black people are best at sport or music careers.

- You sound white. / You don't sound black.

- You speak English really well.

- I don't notice people's colour.

- You're not Irish; you're just a 'plastic paddy'.

Towards female employees

- Now you have children, you'll inevitably be less career-focused.

- As you have a young family, I didn't think you'd want the extra responsibility

- It's fantastic that you've raised three kids and progressed so far in your career!

- Do you ever feel guilty about leaving your children to be looked after by other people?

- Your husband/partner has a good job; do you need to work?

- Successful women find it harder to get or keep a partner.

- Didn't you want to have children?

- We need someone in the role who can make tough decisions.

- Why are you getting so emotional about this?

- I didn't think a woman would be interested in this role.

- You are so attractive; it's hard for people to take you seriously.

- Kelly, could you take the meeting notes for us/ get the coffees for the meeting?

Towards LGBT+ employees

- When did you know you were gay/ lesbian/ trans?

- Were your parents/ family members upset/ disappointed when you 'came out'/ 'reassigned?'

- If you're not a man or a woman, what are you then?

- Have you had surgery?/ Will you have surgery?

- Is this just a phase?

- Who plays the male/ female role in your relationship?

- You're bisexual; does that make your partner feel insecure?

- S/he is not gay/ lesbian. They're normal.

- You're very pretty for a lesbian.

- You don't act gay.

- It's such a waste you're gay/ lesbian.

- That is so gay!

- Gay men are so fashionable/ creative.

Towards employees who have a faith

- You're not like most Muslims/ Sikhs/ Catholics/ Jews.

- In your culture/ community, aren't women expected to obey their husband?

- A lot of Muslim women only go to University to be a better marriage prospect; they don't intend to work. Is that what you're doing?

- Don't you get very hot wearing all those clothes?

- Will you have an arranged marriage?

- Don't you have to marry someone who is the same religion?

- You're so open-minded for someone from your faith.

Towards disabled people

- You are so brave.

- I couldn't inject myself every day. How do you cope?

- I read that xx is really good for your condition. Have you tried it?

- Will you ever get better?

- Can you have an operation to help you see/ hear/ walk?

- Can I pray for you?

- Don't you miss skiing/ running/ playing the piano?

- You're using that chair for sympathy, I've seen you walking.

- You're taking that parking space from someone who really needs it.

Towards younger/older people

- Employing a manager/ contractor who is just out of nappies isn't going to work.

- The team wouldn't take instructions from someone your age.

- You'll understand when you've had a bit more life experience.

- Do you want me to help you with that iPhone/ tablet/ laptop/ new program?

- I think it's great you still work/ drive/ walk to work/ cycle to work.

- We need someone who is digitally native

  ...and speaking slowly to an older person.

Appendix C: Frivolous, vexatious and malicious complaints

Frivolous complaints

These are complaints of harassment or bullying that employees bring to you that have no serious purpose or value. They relate to an issue that is trivial or meritless. If you did carry out an investigation, it would be disproportionate in terms of time and cost. Here are some examples:

Examples

- "My manager is bullying me. He expects me to get to work for 9 am so I can answer the phone at reception. It's difficult for me – I'm not a morning person."

- Bill is harassing me because he opens the window and I prefer it closed."

Vexatious complaints

These are claims or complaints of harassment or bullying that are pursued to annoy or cause problems to you or your organisation.

Example

"My manager put me onto a performance improvement plan because I was missing deadlines. I think he only did that because I'm a woman. I made a harassment complaint. It wasn't upheld by the organisation which annoyed me. Now I tell as many people as I can that he is sexist and undermines women."

Malicious complaints

Complaints which are filed with malicious intent, ie an intention to harm the recipient.

An employer can take disciplinary action against an employee who makes a malicious complaint in the workplace.

Example

"My colleague and I applied for the same job as the team leader. She got the job even though I have more experience.

During my review with the head of department, I told him that she bullies me. She shouts and swears at me when we are working alone. And she always gives me the worst jobs. He advised me to make a complaint so that it could be investigated. I have just made a formal complaint. It's not true, but it's her word against mine."

Good faith

The example above is different from a complaint made by an employee 'in good faith'.

A complaint made in good faith is when your employee genuinely believes their complaint is valid even if it seems malicious or vexatious to you as their manager or employer.

Appendix D: Facilitated meeting – the questions template

(Based on Alan Sharland's excellent *book How to Resolve Bullying in the Workplace: Stepping Out of the Circle of Blame to Create an Effective Outcome for All*)

Background: Teresa has complained about Jon, her manager bullying her (example A) and Soraya, her colleague undermining her (example B).

Questions for Teresa, the person alleging bullying/ undermining

Example A: Bullying by Jon: Please think about the things that have happened, or what Jon has done which you say are bullying and then answer the following questions. (Answers can be written down or just 'kept in your head').

Example B: Undermining by Soraya: Please think about the things that have happened, or what Soraya has done which you say are undermining and then answer the following questions. (Answers can be written down or just 'kept in your head').

Q1: "What has Jon done/ Soraya done, that concerns/ upsets you?"

Discourage Teresa from using words or descriptions that label rather than describe the behaviour, eg

- "Jon *bullies* me" or

- "Soraya *undermines* me in meetings."

Encourage Teresa to be more specific and describe the actual behaviour she experienced which concerned or upset her. For example,

Example A: "Jon *bullies* me" becomes:

"When I make a mistake in my work or haven't finished work on time, Jon discusses it at my desk. He raises his voice, so other team members hear what is said, which embarrasses me."

Example B: "Soraya *undermines* me in meetings" becomes:

"In the team meeting, I suggested ways to improve customer service, and Soraya made a snorting noise and rolled her eyes. When I tried to explain what I meant, she interrupted me. Then she talked over me saying, 'We tried that before and it didn't work'."

Q2: "What would you like Jon to do instead/ Soraya to do instead?"

Example A: "If you make a mistake, how would you prefer Jon to raise it with you?"

Please say more than, "Not shout at me anymore."

"I'd rather you spoke to me in private, away from the team. I would prefer you to explain where I made a mistake calmly without raising your voice. When you shout, I freeze and can't concentrate on what you are saying."

Example B: "What would you prefer Soraya to do in team meetings if she disagrees with your suggestions?"

Please say more than "Stop undermining me."

"I would prefer you to wait until I've finished speaking before you respond. If you disagree with my idea, I would like you to explain why it is not a good suggestion, so I know for the future."

"I would prefer it if you did not make snorting noises and roll your eyes to other people in the meeting as I feel belittled when you do that."

Q3: "What would be a better way of dealing with these situations for you in the future?"

"What would help you with doing that?"

Teresa would suggest a variety of ways that might improve the relationship, such as:

Example A: Jon

"It would help if you sent me an email in advance, explaining what aspect of my work you want to address before discussing it with me face-to-face. Then I'd have time to prepare for the conversation. I get confused when I'm put on the spot."

"I would like you to give me more time to clarify your requirements and ask you questions when you ask me to do a complex piece of work. Then I wouldn't make mistakes or miss deadlines."

Example B: Soraya

"I'd like to discuss my ideas with you one-to-one before we go into meetings. That would help me to understand if they would work. Then I can make more useful suggestions in meetings."

Questions for Jon and Soraya who were accused of bullying/ undermining Teresa.

Please think about the interactions you've had with Teresa and whether there are things you think she may have considered to be bullying or disrespectful behaviour.

You may not see it that way, of course. The purpose of this meeting is not to prove either of you right or wrong, but to help you resolve the issues between you. It's a chance to look at how your working relationship can be improved.

Please consider your answers to the following questions. (Answers can be written down or just 'kept in your head').

Q1: "What actions or behaviours in your working relationship with Teresa do you see as causing difficulties?"

Q2: "What actions or behaviours do you think Teresa may have interpreted as bullying/undermining her?"

- "What was your intention in those behaviours?"

- 'What, if anything, do you feel you could have done differently in those situations?"

194

Q3: "What would be a better way for you of dealing with these situations in the future."

• "What would help you with doing that?"

• "How can you communicate these alternatives for your future working relationship to Teresa?"

• "What would help you with doing that?"

It is crucial that you use 'open' questions which start with:

Who, What, When, Where, Why or How.

This enables each person to create their own answers to their situation.

It will work far better than you suggesting an answer to their situation by saying:

"Could you try…?"

"Would it be a good idea to…?"

These are instructions, not questions. You are leading the person towards a particular solution.

If they don't 'buy into' their own answers, it's unlikely they will carry them out.

Using open questions ensures their answers are genuinely created by them and are not arising from your suggestions or attempts to 'sort it out'.

This will help them to resolve the situation themselves.

When relationships have broken down between your employees, it's tempting to step in and 'fix it', especially if a solution seems obvious to you.

If you step in at this stage, it prevents them from seeing that it is possible to resolve their difficult situation themselves.

Also, they may ask you to step in again if there are problems in their relationship in future.

They need to find ways of improving their future relationship themselves if this is to work long term.

Appendix E: Summary of US and UK investigation processes

US investigation process

Federal harassment laws cover all US employers with 15 or more employees. At least half of US states* also have sexual harassment laws that cover employers with fewer than 15 employees. Where the law applies to your organisation, you are expected to carry out investigations into any claims of harassment, discrimination, or hostile work environment.

If you are a smaller employer, not covered by federal or state laws, you should consider following a similar approach to maintain a safe and productive work environment.

Below is an outline of a typical harassment investigation in a small employer.

State and local laws vary. Employers should verify their compliance requirements with local government agencies.

Complaint received

Your employees can use a variety of methods to report an allegation of harassment, through

- email, letter or voicemail

- an anonymous whistleblower hotline, or even an anonymous note.

You should obtain a detailed, written complaint from the complainant at the outset, whenever possible.

Assess the severity of the claim

When a complaint is received, escalate it to the appropriate internal person within your organisation. This person will verify that it meets, or appears to meet, the legal definition of harassment.

In a large employer, this would be Human Resources, Legal or a designated executive.

In a small employer, the appropriate internal person is likely to be

- the business owner or partner

- a senior manager

- a staff member designated to address these complaints.

Once the claim has been verified as harassment, an investigation is initiated.

You may be the recipient of the initial complaint and the business owner, partner or senior manager. In these circumstances, you should involve a second member of management in the investigation, to ensure impartiality throughout the process.

An impartial individual should be selected to lead the investigation. Their role will include

- coordinating investigatory interviews

- communicating with participants

- keeping superiors apprised of the process.

This individual is referred to as the 'investigation leader' in this summary.

Complaint does not meet the definition of harassment

Your employee may allege harassment, and you conclude their complaint does not fall within the definition.

Their complaint should still be addressed, but a full investigation would not be necessary.

Meeting to discuss claim

If you are the investigation leader you will determine, with input from relevant members of management

- who will be interviewed as a part of the investigation
- who will conduct and document the interviews.

Best practice is for an external investigator, typically an attorney, to conduct interviews and document findings.

However, if this is not viable, you should ask another manager to conduct the interviews.

When the interviewer is an internal employee, you should ensure there are no real or perceived conflicts of interest, eg reporting relationships, personal or familial relationships.

Plan the investigation process

Once the interviewer has been identified, you set up the schedule of interviews. The location must be private, ideally in a place removed from the work area.

Typically, the complainant is interviewed first and the alleged harasser last.

The interviewer creates interview questions for the complainant based upon the content of their complaint. You would assist if required.

Notice of an investigation

You provide the complainant and alleged perpetrator of the harassment with written notice of the investigation.

This should include expectations of confidentiality and policies against retaliation during the process.

Any additional parties with a 'need to know', eg management chain of command or legal team are also notified.

Every effort should be made to keep the complaint and investigation as confidential as possible.

During the investigation, the interviewer may identify additional witnesses to be interviewed.

Consider intermediate measures

You should discuss with relevant managers whether the alleged harasser should be temporarily reassigned or placed on paid administrative leave during the investigation.

Such intermediate measures help to

- reduce the stress on the complainant and
- minimise the risk of retaliatory actions between your two employees.

Conducting interviews

The interviewer conducts each interview, taking detailed notes which are typed up at the end of each session.

Each interviewee is provided with a record of their interview and asked to sign off on the accuracy of their account.

The interviewer prepares interview questions for the alleged perpetrator using the notes from the earlier interviews with the complainant and witnesses.

The alleged perpetrator denies the allegations

The alleged perpetrator may deny the allegations outright. Ask whether they have any documents or witnesses that may support their version of events. If they do, examine the documents they provide and interview their witnesses.

Document investigation results

On completion of all interviews, the interviewer provides a written summary of the results to you as the investigation leader. Depending upon the expertise of the interviewer, their summary may include a recommended course of action.

You review the results and recommend a course of action. You would take into consideration the interviewer's recommendations, if provided.

The results and recommendations are conveyed to the business owner and, if applicable, to appropriate members of management.

If the complaint is upheld, management will recommend, with advice from relevant internal parties, whether to take disciplinary action.

This action may range from a verbal warning to termination. You should have recommendations for termination reviewed by an attorney.

Unable to make a decision

Many harassment claims are "he said, she said". At the end of the investigation, you may have credible yet conflicting statements from the complainant and alleged perpetrator. In these situations, you may be unable to decide who is telling the truth and make a fair and reasonable decision.

As long as you investigate thoroughly and document your findings, you've done your job. If there are any further incidents, you can revisit this file and take a fresh look at the evidence.

Investigation closure

The investigation leader meets with the complainant and provides a brief written notice of the investigation results.

This notice does not include details of disciplinary actions, other than in the case of termination.

The alleged harasser is also provided with a written summary of the investigation results.

Disciplinary actions are documented and may be communicated separately.

All relevant interview notes and investigation documents should be retained in a secure location for at least three years.

UK formal investigation process

Laws on harassment and bullying apply to all UK employers, irrespective of the number of employees.

When carrying out an investigation in the UK:

- Review the initial complaint to ensure it meets the legal definition of harassment or bullying

- Consider separating the complainant and alleged perpetrator during the investigation to

  o   reduce the stress on the complainant

  o   minimise the risk of retaliation between your two employees.

Investigations in the UK are generally carried out by managers internally, rather than an externally sourced solicitor, lawyer or attorney.

Below is a summary of a typical investigation process in a small employer.

Appointment of investigation leader and interviewer

The business owner or a senior manager appoints an investigation leader.

If you are the investigation leader, you will appoint another manager as the interviewer.

You may consult with the owner or senior manager to identify the most suitable person.

The interviewer carries out interviews with all parties involved in the complaint.

Notice of an investigation

The investigation leader provides the complainant and alleged perpetrator of the harassment and bullying with written notice of the investigation.

This should include expectations of confidentiality and policies on victimisation during the process.

The investigation leader sets up the schedule of interviews and advises both parties of the name of the interviewer.

Speak to the complainant first

Full written details of the allegation

If you are the interviewer, ask the complainant to:

- Give full written details of their allegation(s)

- Provide the dates and times of each instance of inappropriate behaviour in their complaint

- Identify any witnesses to these incidents.

Meet with the complainant and witnesses

- Meet with the complainant and go through their complaint to ensure you understand each allegation fully.

- Encourage them to bring a colleague or Trade Union representative to the meeting for support (this is their statutory right so must be offered).

- Speak to any witnesses to the incidents and take notes.

- After each interview, type up the notes.

- Provide each participant with a record of their interview and ask them to sign off on the accuracy of their account.

Notify and interview the alleged perpetrator and their witnesses

- Give the alleged perpetrator written details of the complaint.

- Ask them to respond to each allegation, in writing, stating their recollection of each incident.

- Invite them to a meeting to discuss the complaint with you.

- Encourage them to bring a colleague or Trade Union representative to the meeting for support (this is their statutory right so must be offered).

- Go through each allegation with them and take notes.

- Let them respond and

  o explain their recollection of events

  o give their reasons for behaving in this way

  o provide any mitigating circumstances

  o provide any witnesses to the behaviour.

- Interview any of their witnesses to the alleged behaviour.

- Provide each person with a record of their interview and ask them to sign off the accuracy of their account.

Seek further clarification

- If the accounts of the complainant, perpetrator or any of the witnesses are very different or confusing, seek clarification.

- Invite them to another meeting.

- Ask further questions and/or request additional information where appropriate.

- Update your records if required.

Document investigation results

On conclusion of the interviews, you should provide a written summary to the investigation leader.

In some organisations, you may be asked to recommend a course of action. However, it is usually the investigation leader who makes recommendations.

Either way, all the evidence and the circumstances should be considered carefully before reaching a conclusion.

Unable to make a decision

Many harassment and bullying claims are "he said, she said". At the end of the investigation, you may have credible yet conflicting statements from the complainant and alleged perpetrator. In these situations, you may be unable to decide who is telling the truth and make a fair and reasonable decision.

As long as you investigate thoroughly and document your findings, you've done your job. If there are any further incidents, you can revisit this file and take a fresh look at the evidence.

Making the decision

If you have sufficient evidence and are the person asked to make the decision, ask yourself this question:

'Could what has taken place be reasonably considered to have offended/ humiliated the complainant?'

Make your decision.

If the complaint is upheld, management will recommend, with advice from relevant internal parties, whether to take disciplinary action.

This action may range from a verbal warning to termination.

Investigation closure

The investigation leader meets with the complainant and provides a brief written notice of the investigation results.

This notice does not include details of disciplinary actions, other than in the case of termination.

The alleged perpetrator is also provided with a written summary of the investigation results.

Disciplinary actions are documented and may be communicated separately.

All relevant interview notes and investigation documents should be retained for at least six months.

Complainants in the UK have a 13-week time limit to make a complaint of harassment or bullying against their employer, to an Employment Tribunal.

However, complainants can take civil or criminal action against the individual who perpetrated the harassment or bullying up to six years later. You may wish to retain the records for a more extended period in serious cases.

Right to appeal

Where disciplinary action is taken, you must inform the individual of their right to appeal if they are unhappy with the decision. Provide them with a copy of your appeal process.

After the investigation

In most cases, the perpetrator remains in their job. It is crucial to explore how you will rebuild the relationship between your two employees after the investigation.

It is a good idea to consider access to counselling, mediation, coaching, training or other support for both individuals.

If you are the manager of both employees, you should carry out regular reviews with them individually to ensure there is no victimisation of either person.

Sources of information

Chapter 3: What does the law say about harassment and bullying?

Appendix A: Laws on harassment and bullying

United Kingdom (UK)

Legislation and definitions of harassment and victimisation: Equality and Human Rights Commission www.equalityhumanrights.com

Legislation and definition of bullying: ACAS www.acas.org.uk

Republic of Ireland (ROI)

Legislation and definitions of harassment and victimisation: Irish Human Rights and Equality Commission www.ihrec.ie

Definition of bullying: Labour Relations Committee www.workplacerelations.ie

Legislation and definition of bullying: Health and Safety Authority (ROI) www.hsa.ie

Australia

Legislation and definitions of harassment and victimisation: Australian Human Rights Commission www.humanrights.gov.au and Fair Work Commission www.fwc.gov.au

New Zealand (NZ)

Legislation and definitions of harassment, discrimination and victimisation: Employment New Zealand www.employment.govt.nz

Legislation and definition of bullying: Worksafe New Zealand www.worksafe.govt.nz

Canada

Legislation and definitions of harassment and retaliation: Harassment Canadian Human Rights Commission www.chrc.ccdp.gc.ca

Legislation and definition of bullying: Canadian Centre for Occupational Health and Safety www.ccohs.ca

United States (US)

Legislation and definitions of harassment and retaliation: US Equal Employment Opportunity Commission www.eeoc.gov

Definition of bullying: Workplace Bullying Institute (WBI) www.workplacebullying.org

Legislation and definitions of harassment, bullying and retaliation: 'The Essential Guide to Handling Workplace Harassment and Discrimination' book. Author Deborah C England (Attorney) www.nolo.com

Chapter 4: What behaviours are harassment and bullying

The four main workplace cultures (pages 45-46): Robert E Quinn and Kim S Cameron University of Michigan www.quinnassociation.com

Chapter 12: Mediation and Facilitated Meetings

Appendix D Facilitated Meeting – the question template

'How to Resolve Bullying in the Workplace – Stepping out of the circle of blame to create an effective outcome for all' book. Author Alan Sharland.

Chapter 14: Creating a respectful culture: Manager actions

Active bystander (page 162-166): Tom Relihan 2019 MIT Management Sloan School Article on 'Fixing a toxic work culture.'

Index

Printed in Great Britain
by Amazon